Poetry Ireland Review 103

Eagarthóir/Editor

CAITRÍONA O'REILLY

Poetry Ireland Ltd/Éigse Éireann Teo gratefully acknowledges the assistance of
The Arts Council/An Chomhairle Ealaíon and The Arts Council of Northern Ireland.

Poetry Ireland invites individuals and commercial organisations to become
Friends of Poetry Ireland. For more details please contact:

Poetry Ireland Friends Scheme
Poetry Ireland
2 Proud's Lane
off St Stephen's Green
Dublin 2
Ireland

or telephone +353 1 4789974; e-mail management@poetryireland.ie

PATRONS:
Joan and Joe McBreen

Poetry Ireland Review is published quarterly by Poetry Ireland Ltd. The Editor enjoys
complete autonomy in the choice of material published. The contents of this publication
should not be taken to reflect either the views or the policy of the publishers.

ISBN: 1-902121-41-4
ISSN: 0332-2998

ASSISTANT EDITOR: Paul Lenehan, with the assistance of Adèle Twohig, Haley Davis,
    and David Maybury.
DESIGN: Alastair Keady (**www.hexhibit.com**)
Printed in Ireland by **Brunswick Press Ltd** Unit B2 Bluebell Industrial Estate Dublin 12

Contents   Poetry Ireland Review 103

Derek Mahon

THE ONE-THIRTY

The present generation sees everything clearly.
   – Gogol, *Dead Souls*

The one-thirty p.m. from Petersburg to Moscow
flashes past meadow, Gazprom and dusky forest
lit only by a twilight candle-glow
in the days of revolution and civil war –
a dim vigil for history going sour,
the haunting spectre of a future lost;

and a thicket of aerials up an antique lane.
The ghostly whipped spire of a basilica,
spun blue and white, points to an arctic sky
as in the wilder days of Dostoievsky.
A tiny red light flickers off and on
like somebody smoking at a window-sill

or a plane circling to land at Domodedovo.
No leaves left on suburban maple trees.
At the terminal a chill November breeze,
north-easterly, disperses the first snow,
white flurries hestitating too above
the crimson historic plaza where Lenin lies.

What history? Not the driven ones who work
at the huge desks, not strategy, not the dark
intrigues of the *ne kulturny* oligarch
so much as the slow thought of unknown powers,
wind stirring the wheatfields and wildflowers,
and the recurrent music of exemplars –

old folksong, Glinka and his first tutor
fresh from the west, magician of the keyboard,
tone poet of ice tinkle and frozen rain,
his slight sounds deliberate as thaw water
dropping at night, mysterious Field who 'Dead
in Moscow' from a surfeit of champagne.

Daily frustration and vindictive hunger
only intensified the songbirds' fever,
'Aesopian' in its deeply mined obliquity.
Sun dimmed and garden dripped; funereal weather
waited and listened for their silvery cry.
What doesn't kill you makes you stronger.

Icons, tractors, and this devotional urge
lives on in the profitable post-modern era:
dead souls still glistening like caviare,
the unrealised lives of Black Sea sturgeon
realised finally in a playground song,
miraculous faces of the post-Soviet young.

The last survivors of the difficult years
have faces worn by hardship and lined by tears.
It's thanks to these, the sombre ones who suffered,
that the bright students can sip designer coffee.
'Let's go to the movies!', Voznesensky says;
but films are boring and inane these days.

Luke Morgan

BACK GARDEN

For a place so half-
finished, it's a stand-alone legacy;
there is sorrow to be found
among rained-on garden tools,
damp wood we never used, yet meant to.
There are moments when a teardrop
asks to fall
from the lip of a leaf.

At the rear, an old compost bin
where my father shovelled shit
to clear his head. Lately,
we are still afraid to look inside.

Why am I so passive? Is this not
a memory ahead of me?
Behind,
the future is a question, foul in my mouth
as the past makes haste on crutches,
begging us to stay back.

Jean O'Brien

MERMAN

I had been working in the fish farm for weeks,
that one near the river outlet and the sea.
I didn't like the work we were constantly
wet, dirty, didn't like the men there either.
They were insolent, often dropped small fry
and crushed them underfoot. One in particular
Glaucus, tall, muscular cast his sea-green eyes over me,
tried to lure me as I tipped phosphorus feed
into the holding pens that smoked and stank
and made mist veils I tried to hide within.

One day he walked towards the tanks
waders held in his large hands, he was chewing
on a herb he said was magical, always urging
me to eat it. I would not bite. Anyway whatever way
it was, he leaned to pull the waders on, both legs
got caught in one boot and over he flipped.
I cast around for help, no-one was there. I went back.
He was emerging from amongst the shoals
of salmon, clinging to his single wader
up to his waist were the glittering scales of smolts.

He rose shaking, coloured sequins waterfalling
as he tried to right himself and beckoned me for help.
I took the bait and when I caught him,
we stumbled, he landed me and pinned me down,
I looked, held his eyes, it was early the rising sun
was flooding them with hooks of golden light. I said No.
He parted my thighs and when it was over,
untangled his legs, shook the silver armour
from himself, his eyes had lost their lustre.

I left distraught and walked all day stumbling
over ditches and hillocks, stopped now and then
to eat, following the river to its source.
At so many hundred feet I rested where the stream
welled from the earth, cooled my toes, kicked gravel
into little pools and felt the flow snagging
in the waters of my womb. I cried and screamed
and shook my fists at the sky, knew then this birthing
pool was to be my fate, tried to obliterate
his sea-green eyes, his face, his terrible merman tail.

Winner of the Arvon International Poetry Competition 2010

Kate Dempsey

AMSTERDAM OTTO RECOMMENDS

And an emerald, square cut, says Otto,
green for Ireland or something like that, offset just so.

Diamonds on black felt sparkle under
halogen lamps like a night sky in the polders.

We nod, dazed as the guilders churn
to madness. He tweezers the tiny stone, turns

so it glitters like Elizabeth Taylor's first;
one month's salary in one small burst.

Of course, in a few years, he says, glancing up,
but not at me, you can trade up.

John Redmond

ONCE A CLOUD

Once a cloud
love happens now.
How we evolved
Colosseums ago
is a question
these altocirrus
versions of our
every move
impose, my dear,

blowing overhead.
The evening sky's
a feast of making
where we make out
our unicorn selves,
colossal and slow,
developing holes
like a Henry Moore.

Down here too
where foreplay
is lit by afterglow
the clouds I give you
have nowhere to go,
abridging a future
of indigo shadow:
a softer St Peter's.

Gerard Smyth

THE RUSSIAN DELICATESSEN

When the Russian delicatessen opened
opposite the Chinese takeaway,
I thought of my father and what he might say
to see this strange cuisine displayed
on one of his Dublin streets,
his hunting ground for life's necessities.
A street of apples and oranges,
where books were second-hand.
The quarter mile he walked like an earl
upon his land, up and down, from end to end,
an old habit he kept even when
he became a man of little appetite,
fooled by tricks of memory
and his luck ran out in the Saturday Derby.
A street where he stood on corners
to watch the passing of an age,
stood still to catch his breath at twelve
and six o'clock when the new electric bells
broke into song, an annunciation that made him pause,
straighten his shoulders and then walk on.

Ron Houchin

SUMMER TENANTS

The white spider riding
my shoulder from the reed bush,
like a bit of cotton down,
will not be here long enough

to get to know. The sweat bee
that mines the wet crease
of my neck had hummed through
the door, disoriented as a vacationer
dropping his bag in the vestibule.

From late spring, the neighbourhood could
as well be Cairo, Galway, or Cusco,
full of creatures that come with 'Ninety
Days' stamped on their passports.

I don't begrudge them their itineraries
any more than I do their lives, but
the speed at which they buzz over
my perennials, looking only
at what drew them from some brochure.

Killian O'Donnell

FRESCOS

NOLI ME TANGERE
(Attrib: Fra Angelico)

God says: *I am not yet ascended to the Father.* As though
he assumes the girl – baffled, too petrified to think –

has worked out he's not the gardener but the man she knows
is dead, back from the dead. I shut the guidebook, floored

by dogma, and fall again for how intensely scattered
pimpernels pick up her gown, a maverick drench of pink.

CRUCIFIXION
(Attrib: assistant to Fra Angelico)

Whoever it is is over-descriptive, elaborate, minute, his craft
impeccable, but meek. He depends too much on delicacy

of tone to compensate for the stillborn attack, the never-to-be
pressed-home advantage. There he is, grinding azurite

for the virgin's shawl. In slips the Master. He draws lead-white
from its scabbard. And fleshes it – once, twice – to the haft.

ANNUNCIATION
(Attrib: Fra Angelico)

His virgin comes across touch mousy, his angel unsexed
by gorgeous draperies, wings – that ladyboy hairdo... – so,

don't expect miracles, but one moment to penetrate the next
until conception occurs, and the wholeness of the thing

is triggered – like a pot of apples exploding to apple-snow
or an ash tree in April, every detail clearing its throat to sing.

J S Robinson

MARTHA MAXWELL, MOTHER OF TAXIDERMY

Have you put her body onto the page
nicks and cuts on each hand
the scraping blade,
train vibrations driving up from the sacrum?

All the crystal eyes
held and turned and painted,
the exactness of paint flecks, she licking
a sable tip, yellow and red cadmiums

crossing her tongue.
These softened furs stroked and handled,
she knowing where each was shot,
their bodies left among rocks; for vultures

will come down into her inventions,
theatre of the wild.
Is she in these padded places,
angularities of elbows, boots buttoned

to the knees, dress closed
at the throat, her tight swallowing?
Not mittelschmerz but a flowering of cells,
a hand pressed.

Mary O'Donnell

THE PARTS

Waxen parts observed in the Ethnographic Museum,
Santiago de Compostela, Spain

Let us collect a waxen body part
from the corner-shop just after dawn
before the newspapers are delivered.

An arm for you, a hip for me,
a heart for him, phallus, breast
or tongue. Even if we no longer

believe in a god, and no one in their right mind
believes there is a celestial form
which our ailments will fit,

for the cure of misdreamt bodies,
let us take the waxen parts of the old aunt's
failing limbs, the claw of her paralysed

arm, her frozen right leg,
trembling bottom lip, a tongue
which forgets to close off saliva.

Take her wheelchair also.
It has absorbed the illness,
needs molecular healing.

Take a daughter's S-shaped spine,
the scar tissue on her left lung,
let us bear the knots of the fish-monger's arthritis,

his pinched feet and short, hot tendons,
lay them in wax on an operating table,
where belief in a god is not required.

Take our parts in wax. Lay them
as a sign that multitudinous fragments –
hanging hearts and phalluses, used-up wombs,

legs, arms and spines – may despite all rise as one,
to be read and marvelled at
even before the newspapers are delivered.

Lynley Edmeades

CARRY-ON

'In these English-speaking-islands
it means commotion, hullabaloo,

Shakespeare's *much ado.*'
That wasn't what I had in mind,

but I go along with it anyway.
We'd been talking about the sun,

how it moves around the house
regardless. That kind of carry-on.

Annemarie Ní Churreáin

PROTEST

One cut and the hair worn since childhood
fell upon the floor
dead soft.

A spear-thistle;
her new, bald skull
refused order.

She belonged to heather
and in tail-streams
cupping frogs,

delighting
in the small, green pulse of life
between palms,

not here:
at the dark centre of reunions, separations,
starved of air.

This was a protest of love, against love
demanding
sun, rain, wilderness.

From a finger, she slid a band
placed it underfoot,
pressed down

until the stone
made the sound of a gold chestnut
cracking open.

Stuart Barnes

FINGAL

It was much the same as any other
redneck town: more pubs
than happy marriages, a burdened
but voiceless main road, at least one homo-
sexual without a choice.

Along its potholed highway witchy
copses of gorse, perhaps a carcass
(kangaroo, Devil, Major Mitchell), and willows
that wept their barbed and zealous roots
into the Esk.

Its men mined coal or raped
the conifers planted in pretty, crossed rows,
its women bitched and swapped
recipes for wild black swan and sickly-sweet jams as freely
as they swapped barbiturates;

their children, born with a stubbie of home-
brew in one hand and
a slug gun in the other, lazed
away the days like fattening pigs
in above-ground pools

riddled with the larvae of shiny black beetles
or in the oily glow from TV screens
that showed R-rated violence
and XXX sex rented from the wife-beater boar
at the video store.

Each day an inferno, Cerberus
picking the meat from my bones,
each night magnifying, possessed
by at least one more falling
star than the last.

At thirteen, after a lifetime
of Christmases, Easters and Sundays'
black masses, I unrolled the scrolls to my
Torah, and swore to my psychotic father
a bloody and public suicide.

Stuart Barnes

UPON DIAGNOSIS

you hauled the crude nails in between
the bones of your wrists and feet –
the pain was exquisite as living;

then, hoisting the crucifixion to the sandalwood
rosary hanging from Castor and Pollux,
you cried out to no God but yourself

'how could I have been so fucking stupid.'
A crow, passing over, gobbled the useless
rhetoric from among the particles

of air that were colliding like comets and,
perching on your shoulder, nibbled
three times at your earlobe; the collarbone

clawed the Victorian pearls.
The crow departed, but only after sleeking
your cheek with its glossy headdress;

that was all you needed
to slip from the temporary necklace
and into free fall

through a mid-August flurry,
the most exquisite flakes
thawing on your tongue.

Hallucinating fish,
you landed on your childhood tricycle;
fractals swirled in the snowdrifts

as you peddled toward
a mountain of crimson stone
which revealed, amid its evergreen

foothills, the mouth to a cave
empty except for a loaf of sourdough,
a first edition of *The Secret History*,

and a Mamiya RB67, with film;
you serenely rolled its boulder into place.
The crow, from its conifer, watched over.

Edward Reilly

LEICESTER: JULY

Across the road there's a house with a yellow door,
Two geranium bushes growing on the front grass
Mown a few days earlier in the week, a rosebush,
Unusual for the lazy line of developer-cottages,
And I am struck at the untidiness of the streetscape
Quite unlike that of the smaller towns on the Continent
Where I had been the fortnight beforehand, scruffy almost,
And a bus stop about twenty paces downhill, just like today,
Everything left unsaid, like the disordered state of the loungeroom,
Books and CDs scattered everywhere, boxes of pills,
Emulsions to ease belly cramps, half-eaten crisps:
I turn off the power to the television, which no one regards
While the two bespoke consuls of the State wave
As the crowd waves back, the Queen is rather regal,
Smiling now that order is restored to this insular realm.

The coffee is bitter. There's a score for Cage's prepared pianos
Jammed next to copies of Brahms and Bach's *Kinderbuch*,
Garner's novel is surely buried away on the shelf
Next to Baiba Skride & the Munich Philharmonic,
Schostakowitsch's violin concerto, #1/77 – 99, now appearing
In the repertoire, perhaps more often than Tschaikowsky:
I wonder what Oistrach would say after those delicate years
When his friend was living behind closed doors,
This slip of a lassie from the grey Baltic shores
Weeping for all that has gone before, and will come after:
The kitchen table is awash with daily ordinaries,
There's a fold of bank-notes, Euros and Swiss Francs,
A letter with an Australian stamp, a card from Deutschland,
Sermons given at Doncaster, neatly arranged in stacks,
Devotional literature and dictionaries of Mathematics.

Green grass, a children's swing, ladder & slide, painted bench,
Two women watching a lone child dawdling,
Flowers, *impatiens* perhaps, massed in baskets by a brick wall
Which seems to have been the side of a factory,
Rustbelt made habitable, a newspaper left behind,
More out of forgetfulness, one surmises, its pages folded

For the reader to return later in the day, but he hasn't:
We have unhitched your bicycle and stored it here,
Next to the files of music scores and your books.
A birch tree begins to dance in the afternoon light.
Then a bus passes by the front window, brakes flaring
As it fights gravity, avoiding two children on skates,
A car pulls up next door, doors slam, girlish laughter
Rings across the street and up the hill to the commons.
Your mother tries to be optimistic. She'll stay on.

Thomas Dillon Redshaw

MY FATHER'S FEET

He props himself up at the edge of his painted bed,
Arms angled out, hand holding the mattress's edge.
I have lotion and a towel on the floor beside me.
He has a lot to say about the strain of bending
Unsteadily to clip his nails, care for his feet
On his own.
                    Kneeling in front of him,
I rub the lotion between my palms and take
One white foot at a time, ankle and toes, easing
The tendons, then palm each heel, each narrow sole
Again and again, letting him catch the lotion's scent
Of rosemary.
                    On the bed's grained headboard
In faded gold and black someone once stenciled
A dim theorem of a cornucopia spilling out
Apples, melons, grapes. This is the least I can do.

Thomas Dillon Redshaw

FLOATERS

In the yellow flash of a blink
Hermes stands, just off to the right
Of the eye & free of the instant flare
Of dark capillaries.
                        He is quick.
His beckoning slight, erased
By daylight, lamplight that floods
The page of sight with a detail there
That draws & draws again the focus
Of breath.
                What catches the breath
Upon closer look looks like
A sentence written round the clear
Orbit of the pupil & again round
The unfurled colour of the iris.

Kerry Hardie

QUESTIONS

I think my perinatal bone's re-opening
and I have whizzed out through the soft hole in my head.
I have such thoughts – the doors have all flown wide.
My furniture's been moved outside, it shines with rain.

Is this what growing up is really all to do with?
This flying through the air and turning inside out?
Who said I was a house with beds and tables,
with dining chairs and cabinets and parquet floors?

I search out doorways opening onto courtyards,
and from the courtyards, arches onto fields.
Each holds a presence in the shape of absence
that's like the empty smell that follows rain.

So who is telling me that I need furniture,
or that it matters if my house is sound?
Why did I listen when I told myself I knew the answers?
Who made me think I'll end up dead after I've died?

S D Tucker

GREAT MINDS THINK ALIKE

S D Tucker explores the origins and nature of Yeats's peculiar model of the poetic imagination, and how he viewed it as being a common legacy for all future Irish poets.

In 1926, two books with wildly different themes were published; *A Vision* by W B Yeats, which purported to be a record of the author's experiments with spiritualism and automatic writing, and the first English translation of the German writer Oswald Spengler's self-explanatorily titled *Decline of the West*. In both books, however, there was a small similarity; the difference between Greek and Roman thought had been symbolised by both authors in terms of the difference between the blank or painted eyes of ancient Greek statues and the pierced eyeballs of ancient Roman ones.[1]

How could this have happened? Looking at it, most people would regard this similarity as being mere coincidence. Others, more mystically inclined, may prefer to bring in telepathy. To the author of one of those two works, however, W B Yeats, the similarity in imagery was to be explained by nothing less than the fact that both writers must have had access to a kind of 'great mind', existing in some kind of disembodied state in nature, in which the image was stored, entire and complete, before it had actually been written down by them. This 'great mind', to Yeats, was nothing less than the *anima mundi*, or 'soul of the world' as had been described by the ancient Neoplatonist philosophers, and was conceived of by him as being a great, infinite storehouse of images and ideas just waiting to be tapped into by those who were most attuned to the idea – people like mystics, visionaries ... and poets.

It seems, on first sight, to be an unreasonable explanation for such a minor similarity; but not for Yeats. By the time of *A Vision*'s publication, the poet had long been convinced of the necessity of the *anima mundi*'s existence; indeed, his entire model of what might be termed 'the poetic imagination' had been essentially modelled upon it. But why? For an answer to this, we need to go back to Yeats's youth, when he came under the influence of a strange Scotsman named MacGregor Mathers, a prominent member of the Hermetic Order of the Golden Dawn, and a man utterly obsessed with occult matters.

A co-founder of the Dublin Hermetic Society himself in 1885, Yeats initially proved an eager disciple for Mathers, though they later quarrelled, and it was through him that the poet first began to become convinced of the existence of some kind of 'great mind' in nature. Mathers was soon getting Yeats to engage in certain mystical experiments with him, and it was during one of these that he first claimed to have encountered the *anima mundi*. Holding a wooden mace and making use of a table full of coloured squares and numbers, Mathers proceeded to repeat a form of magical incantation. 'Almost at once,' wrote Yeats later, in his work *Magic*, 'my imagination began to move of itself and to bring before me vivid images that, though never too vivid to be imagination, as I had always understood it, had yet a motion of their own, a life I could not change or shape ...' [2]

Here, Yeats sounds initially hesitant. He does still seem to think there is a possibility that it was all 'just' imagination that Mathers was inducing in him, even if it did seem to have a life of its own. However, with other sitters, Yeats soon began experiencing *shared* visions that seemed to have been brought about by Mathers's influence. His initial instinct was to blame telepathy. Other experiments with Mathers changed his mind.

For example, Mathers once handed Yeats a symbol taken from the ancient Jewish Kabbalah and drawn on cardboard, and told him to close his eyes. Apparently, this induced a significant mystical experience in Yeats: 'Sight came slowly ... there rose before me images that I could not control; a desert and black Titan raising himself up by his two hands from the middle of a heap of ancient ruins. Mathers explained that I had seen a being of the order of Salamanders because he had shown me their symbol'.[3] This is significant as, according to this explanation, it was not Mathers himself who was causing Yeats to have the vision, via telepathic influence, but rather the inherent power of the symbol itself. If the cabalistic symbol had been shown to another person with some kind of visionary capacities, then they too would have seen the salamander-type creature and not some other kind of entity. It seemed now to Yeats, then, that certain images were stored away somewhere, unseen, and could be conjured up in the human mind by the contemplation of certain apparently powerful corresponding symbols.

Further evidence for this idea came to Yeats when he observed a young Irishwoman who, during her waking state 'thought the apple of Eve was the kind of apple you can buy at the greengrocer's' but, when passing into a mystical trance, saw 'the Tree of Life with ever-sighing souls moving in its branches instead of sap, and among its leaves all the fowls of the air, and on its highest bough one white fowl wearing a crown.' Going home, Yeats cut the pages on an unread copy of Mathers's *The Kabbalah Unveiled*, and found an account of that same tree which broadly corresponded with the young girl's vision. A bank clerk from the west of Ireland was also witnessed by Yeats having a similar vision; only he saw apples with human faces and found, to his great surprise, that the garden of Eden was walled and sat on top of a great mountain, contrary to his expectations. Yeats later found a medieval diagram which depicted Eden as being just such a place.[4]

These ordinary, common folk could not, Yeats reasoned, have been expected to have been aware of such incredibly obscure pre-existing mystical images which were themselves to be found only in books of correspondingly extreme obscurity. Therefore, he felt, they had to be accessing them from some kind of great mental storehouse such as the *anima mundi*. But, if this were so, where did these images come from, exactly? How did they get to be in the *anima mundi* in the first place? Yeats seems to have had mixed ideas about this matter. Sometimes, he appears to have felt that they were simply in there, pre-existing human conscious-ness entirely, in a manner not unlike Jung's archetypes. At other times, he concludes that 'whatever the passions of man have gathered about' becomes a symbol in the racial memory of mankind, and can thus later be summoned up by those who know how.[5] If this were so, of course, then it would have meant that the storehouse of images could be altered and added to by the truly poetic and imaginative man – a fact which would be of great importance to him later.

However, Yeats's particular conception of the *anima mundi* was some-what different from that of certain Neoplatonists in a few key ways. One reason for this was the fact that, after he married Georgie Hyde-Lees in 1917, his young wife began going into trances and producing reams and reams of occult philosophy from a series of spirit guides who termed themselves 'Instructors', and who seemed to have been living, somehow, within the *anima mundi* itself. The exact philosophy these entities imparted is far too complex to go into in detail here, but seemed to include as a part of it the notion that certain of the dead themselves still existed somehow within the *anima mundi*, at least for a while. If this was so, thought Yeats, then perhaps they could be contacted. As he wrote in *Per Amica Silentia Lunae*, 'Communication with *anima mundi* is through the association of thoughts or images or objects; and the famous dead, and those of whom but a faint memory lingers, can still ... tread the corridor and take the empty chair.'[6]

It is important to realise that Yeats does not just mean this metaphori-cally. To him, the spirits of the 'famous dead' really could be conjured up from their resting place in *anima mundi* and made in some sense to live again, if only people would contemplate the correct and necessary symbols to do so. One such set of symbols was that which could be found in poetry. Just like Mathers had conjured up visions in Yeats via magical incantations, the words and symbols in poetry could also be viewed as having magical properties which enabled the dead to be, if not exactly literally *resurrected*, then at least *reaccessed* by the living. There is a sense in which poems, then, were a kind of magical spell to Yeats. They could 'call down among us certain disembodied powers, whose footsteps over our hearts we call emotions', as he wrote in *The Symbolism of Poetry*.[7] In this way, he felt that poets, musicians and artists were in fact the modern successors of the old 'masters of magic' of the past, people like Swedenborg and Cornelius Agrippa.[8]

However, there was a problem with accessing the minds of the dead within the *anima mundi*; once they had passed into it they seemed to become increasingly incoherent and almost, for want of a better word, senile. It was not, then, possible to just 'summon up' Dante for a chat somehow. This is how Yeats described the state of souls stuck in the *anima mundi* waiting to be reborn in his poem *The Phases of the Moon*:

> ... they speak what's blown into the mind,
> Deformed beyond deformity, unformed,
> Insipid as the dough before it is baked.

You may, in some sense, be able to access dead poets and artists and the beautiful images that they carry together with them up there in *anima mundi*, then, but you can't really expect to, for example, get some full and complete new poetry from out of them. Instead, that is the job of the living poet. By reading great poetry from the past, you might well be able to access some images from *anima mundi* which were made use of by that poet, or, indeed, get in contact with what little remains of that poet himself in the afterlife, but these dead poets will not in themselves be creative as, apparently, 'even the most wise dead can but arrange their memories as we arrange pieces upon a chess-board and obey remembered words alone'.[9] Therefore, then, it is the job of the living poet to access these 'memories', or images, of the old poets, and then rearrange and combine them in new ways, to work upon them and make them new in some sense, in order to rescue images of beauty from out of the *anima mundi* and bring them back with him into this world, refashioned anew, like some kind of shaman, perhaps. Yeats's 'Instructors' may well have told him that 'we have come to give you metaphors for poetry'[10], but perhaps it would have been more accurate for them to say that they came to bring him certain symbols which then had to be *crafted* into metaphors for use in his poetry. This is actually the explanation for the poet's self-imposed hard-labour as famously described by Yeats in *Adam's Curse*:

> ... A line will take us hours maybe;
> Yet if it does not seem a moment's thought,
> Our stitching and unstitching has been naught.

He gives an example of the results of this labour in *The Symbolism of*

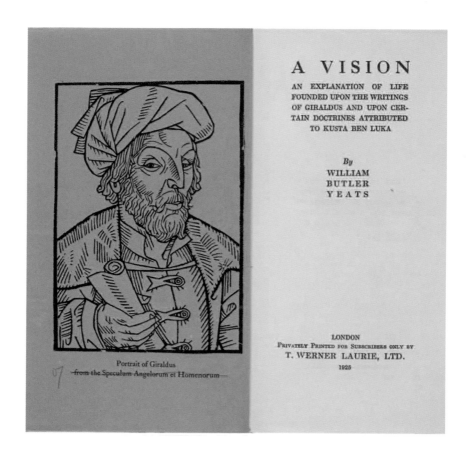

Portrait of Giraldus
from the Speculum Angelorum et Homenorum

A VISION

AN EXPLANATION OF LIFE
FOUNDED UPON THE WRITINGS
OF GIRALDUS AND UPON CER-
TAIN DOCTRINES ATTRIBUTED
TO KUSTA BEN LUKA

By
WILLIAM
BUTLER
YEATS

LONDON
PRIVATELY PRINTED FOR SUBSCRIBERS ONLY BY
T. WERNER LAURIE, LTD.
1925

A Vision, dated 1925, appeared in January 1926

Image courtesy of the National Library of Ireland

'This notebook was kept by William Butler Yeats from 1893, when he entered the Inner Order of the Golden Dawn, to 1912, when the Order had ceased to call itself the Golden Dawn following various public scandals.'

'The section of the notebook shown is copied from a document by MacGregor Mathers, explaining how to build up the visible form of a name representing an elemental force.'

Image and text courtesy of the National Library of Ireland

Thoor Ballylee, near Gort, Co Galway

George Hyde-Lees (Georgie) and William Butler Yeats with their children Anne and Michael

Image courtesy of the National Library of Ireland

Poetry, when he speaks of Burns's line 'The white moon is setting behind the white wave' being a metaphor for mortality and the passing of time. Here, various images which take their power ultimately from their existence as *images* (rather than as the things they actually are) in the *anima mundi* – the moon, the waves, and whiteness – are combined together creatively in order to generate both a metaphor and an image of beauty. Literally, for Yeats, this is an act of creative magic; together, these symbols have combined to conjure up beauty into our world from out of the immortal realm.[11]

Another way to put this, if you are not a spiritualist, might be to say that it is the poet's job to rescue unconscious contents from the unconscious, consciously alter them in some way, and then make them appear as if they were unconscious again. It is a hard thing to do – I think we can all think of certain poems in which the thought-processes involved in its writing are all-too obvious to the reader – and, for Yeats, it came to seem that it was the level of unconscious quality of the symbolism contained within a work of art which acted as an ultimate arbiter of its quality, providing a kind of path through to a direct experience with the godhead, as he discusses in his work *Symbolism in Painting*: 'All art that is not mere story-telling, or mere portraiture, is symbolic,' he says, having the purpose of 'entangling, in complex colours and forms, a part of the Divine Essence.'[12]

That phrase 'mere' is very telling; if something is 'mere portraiture', for example, he means that it is purely representational – a painting of a face which is nothing more than a depiction of a face. A symbolic work of art, however, has by its very nature many meanings attached to it, as it springs ultimately from *anima mundi* and so the exact nature of its power must remain at least partially unknowable. This quality, of providing access to the unknowable, the numinous, is what makes a great poem, says Yeats in *The Philosophy of Shelley's Poetry*: 'It is only by ancient symbols, by symbols that have numberless meanings beside the one or two the writer lays an emphasis upon ... that any highly subjective art can escape from the barrenness and shallowness of a too conscious arrangement, into the abundance and depth of nature.'[13]

It is significant that this statement was made during a discussion of the symbolism of towers within Shelley's work; because Yeats's own poem, *The Tower*, is one of his works which best exemplifies his quasi-Neoplatonist beliefs. The tower referred to in the piece's title, of course, was Thoor Ballylee, a small Norman castle near Coole where he ended up living after his marriage to Hyde-Lees. This structure was used as a kind of 'living symbol' for Yeats during his occupancy; it was not merely a literal tower of stone and wood, but also, simultaneously, carried all of the resonance of the *poetic image* of the tower in both literature and the 'great mind'. Indeed, seeing as the literal tower shares to a degree in its simultaneous symbolic existence elsewhere for him, there is a sense in which it actually has a kind of soul. For example, during his poem Yeats speaks of 'certain men-at-arms',

> Whose images, in the Great Memory stored,
> Come with loud cry and panting breast
> To break upon the sleeper's rest
> While their great wooden dice beat on the board.

According to Yeats, these ghosts of ancient soldiers playing dice had actually been seen in his own bedroom – but, apparently, they were not merely shades of the unquiet dead, but some kind of phantom embodiment of the tower's potential symbolic contents.[14] If Thoor Ballylee was a kind of 'living symbol', however, then it seems as though Yeats saw himself as being its resident magician. In *The Phases of the Moon*, Yeats has two late-night passers-by look up and see him at work by candle-light through his castle's window – 'An image of mysterious wisdom won by toil' – and describe him as being like 'Milton's Platonist' sat up late at night in his own tower. This reference is to Milton's *Il Penseroso*, which also describes a mystical Neoplatonist-type who is still sat up and hard at work at the midnight hour, the relevant lines of which read:

> ... let my lamp at midnight hour
> Be seen in some high lonely tow'r,
> Where I may oft outwatch the Bear,
> With thrice-great Hermes, or unsphere
> The spirit of Plato to unfold
> What worlds or what vast regions hold
> The immortal mind that hath forsook
> Her mansion in this fleshly nook.

This, then, is what Yeats saw himself as being during his stay in Thoor Ballylee – a kind of living symbol himself, both participating in, and also to a degree embodying, the ancient poetic conceit or symbol of the seeker after hidden knowledge, as appears, for instance, in Milton's poem. In fact, these lines of *Il Penseroso* also relate to Yeats's beloved Neoplatonist-like concepts in other ways, too. Plato himself is here depicted as being able to be conjured back down from out of the *anima mundi* – 'unsphered' meaning that he is called down from the heavens, or 'spheres' – by some kind of magical, hermetic activity, just like Yeats thought could happen with the 'famous dead' through the reading of their poems. Importantly also, the poet (or hermeticist) himself is seen as participating in some way in the *anima mundi*, even whilst he is still alive; an 'immortal mind' has 'forsook her mansion' in his mind and body, 'this fleshly nook'. There is a sense, then, in which the 'great soul' of the *anima mundi* finds itself enfleshed within the temporary fleshly body of man whilst he still breathes, and that the two participate in one another thereby.

If this were true, then it might also be the case that a living poet – such as Yeats – might in some way be able to influence his later spiritual form in the *anima mundi* by the way in which he lives his life or writes his work. He could try, for example, to fill it full of symbols, through whose contemplation future generations might somehow be able to 'bring him back' to them in some sense. As he writes in *The Tower*, 'Now shall I make my soul'; and there is certainly a degree to which his later poetry is an attempt by him to fashion some kind of means of communication between himself and a future generation of (primarily Irish) poets and readers which is to be made use of when he inhabits the *anima mundi* himself once he is dead. Look, for example, at these lines from *The Tower*:

> As at the loophole there
> The daws chatter and scream,
> And drop twigs layer upon layer.
> When they have mounted up,
> The mother bird will rest
> On their hollow top,
> And so warm her wild nest.

Compare this now with a statement Yeats makes in *Per Amica Silentia Lunae*: 'The dead living in their memories are, I am persuaded, the source of all that we call instinct ... and it is the dream martens that, all unknowing, are master-masons to the living martens building about church windows their elaborate nests'.[15] The inclusion of these lines about the daws are significant in a poem in which Yeats seems to be much-concerned with the legacy he and his work are leaving for the next generation, as the act of building a nest can be seen as a metaphor for many things – continuity, poetic heritage, the continual building and then rebuilding of an entire civilisation, even. It is a comforting image, of unity and wholeness. And yet – how is it that these birds know how to build their nests? Are they taught by older birds or is it just hard-wired into them? For Yeats, the answer is that they know through a kind of instinct inherited from their ancestors, the 'dream martens', living on now in the *anima mundi*. The symbol of the nest conjures up the ability to build it through the living birds' contemplation of it, apparently.

It is the same with nations, too, and, here, with Irish culture and poetic heritage. For the future generations of Irish poets, Yeats seems to suggest, he will be 'the mother-bird', from his position in the 'great mind', helping them to construct their art from beyond the grave. As long as his poems, and the symbols which he has encoded within them – the rose, for instance, the sidhe, or the 'rough beast' of *The Second Coming* – are read and engaged with, or, even better, are remade and refashioned as new pieces of work, then he will live on as a source of inspiration for all those artists and word-smiths who follow after him. To Yeats, his poetry seems to have been a means, quite literally, of keeping himself alive through interaction between it and eternity. Of course, the reader may choose not to *literally* believe this himself – but it is at least true through metaphor. Yeats is still read, and loved, and engaged with, very widely indeed. He has, no doubt, been an inspiration for many other poets who came after him. In this sense at least, then, his strange philosophies really were true, whether in a literalistic sense or not. The great man really does live on still, through his work – and who of us could really hope for any more?

References
I have made use of the Oxford World's Classics edition, *W B Yeats: The Major Works* (2001), for access to both the prose works and poems, with occasional reference to the Everyman edition, *WB Yeats: The Poems* (1992), for further specific details.

1 Oxford p.437
2 Oxford p.345
3 Everyman, p.619-620
4 Oxford, p.346
5 Oxford, p.349
6 Oxford, p.421
7 Oxford, p.360
8 Oxford, p.349
9 Oxford, p.420
10 Oxford, p.431
11 Oxford, p.360
12 Oxford, p.356
13 Oxford, p.351
14 Everyman, p.637
15 Oxford, p.420

Paul Perry

THE RED FOREST

I.

I went there too
I did not have to go
I saw the best of men

clearing the villages was awful
we hated ourselves for that
in the streets we found

maddened cows dripping
with milk
bellowing in pain

it was something terrible
I saw a cat in a window
I thought it was an ornament

then I saw that it was alive
I killed the cat
I got used to killing

forgive us
we found notes nailed
to the doors of houses

be careful we'll be back
don't kill our cat
our house we are sorry

for leaving you
cold and alone
I came home

my wife was frightened
she insisted I throw my clothes away
I did that

all except for my hat
it had a badge on the front
and my son I knew would like it

he was proud of me
he went around wearing this hat
some nights he wore it in bed

one year after that time
he fell ill
it was a brain tumour

that was it
I can say
no more

II.

I dream about it every night
we arrived at 6 a.m.
we told them to leave everything

they cried
as if they knew
they would never return

they offered us moonshine
everything was negotiable
we bartered cattle

they were sold cheap
Nature was dying
the houses were like works of art

empty now
the shadow of madness
was on us all

III.

we lifted the topsoil

the burial grounds were open pits

we stripped the earth and orchards

do not have children they told us

at night we drank

we drank hard

we slept in beds of straw

IV.

we gathered at the train station
it was May
we had been chosen

our work was secret
the mood was fun
we were conscripts

and were called tourists
from the trains we saw the fields
change from green

to something more lunar
white dolomite sand covered
miles of field where the green

earth had once been
we knew then something
was very wrong

the roofs had the names of women
Katya Natasha Anna
Marsha was the mad one

she was cut open like a wound
we stopped laughing
after we arrived in hell

V.

they bent to the water
but did not drink

VI.

the garden all dressed
in wedding white
my hives over there

under the apple trees
I said to Nina my wife
what's wrong

I put on my mask
and checked
they were there

sitting in the hives
not making a sound
there was no buzzing

so strange was their silence

VII.

the rain was black
and one by one the children fell
I will never forget the mornings

the girls had ribbons in their hair
the boys wore shorts
inside I am empty

I have seen and heard too much
I was happy once
the children came from love

our lives are a long winter
without Spring
we bury the children's clothes in dirt

VIII.

we came carrying birch and rowan

a storm broke

dust entered our mouths and eyes

like a black wing

we went on singing

the rivers are our enemies

picking strawberries is not allowed

or bluebells or daisies or mushrooms

the village is buried

in a bitter dream

John McAuliffe

MARRIAGE, THE REALIST TRADITION

There are introductions. A letter arrives. Already
we sympathise with the solitary reader, the interrupted study
in a house no one visits. Who would want to?
We are gripped by an idea, a pilgrimage turns into
a road trip. In the awful weather monsters shrink and, indoors,
assume human forms. We might grow into these foyers and porches.
Where were we? The twin no one ever knew returns.
A mysterious stranger's glance means a head turns.
It is a gaze we follow; now, an inheritance or marriage
is in the balance. New laws or wars throw a shadow, like knowledge,
on what used to happen, but won't ever happen again. Is this
the improbable lift-off into another world, like and unlike life?
Illness sudden as eclipse, or that famous intervention,
love, makes impossible a life of their own invention.
A misunderstanding, a wrong name taken to heart?
No place here for the bad student considering art
but the novelists, the last to specialise in everything, produce
with the frenzy of an enormous unselfconscious youth
a city like a farm, and characters with something to say or
something to hide, and later, a dénouement, on the moor
or in the car park, foreshadowed with subtle hints, maybe this
the improbable lift-off into another world, like and unlike life?
Someone's paying attention to the weather, its big picture;
there is an etymological diversion, an old man (someone's father?)
who retells or invents (will they, won't they?) the monstrous past.
A letter arrives, stop describing the clock – her mother's: open it!
We sit around a table, old and flat and round,
waiting for the girls and the boys to arrive, then head in hand,
no longer talking, we're discovered by the same old story. The plot
creaks into place around us, a picture frame gilded and ornate,
too neat and a little too close to whatever we call home,
which is where (we saw it coming) she takes his name,
stitching everyone into the same black and white pattern
and, somewhere off the page, an ending we believe in.

John McAuliffe

ADDRESS TO RUSS

True reasons for not making it into the office and doing a day's work on the
hard copy of (then) variously titled manuscript

Kneehigh snow. Though I could have walked it.
Or stayed put. The kids were sick so I had to mind them.
I was sick and confined to bed. The car was stolen.
The front door blew in: I had to guard the house.
I'm waiting for a call from my bank, and my mother.
I'm expecting a delivery. I've been called in to teach,
I had work to catch up on, marking, admin.
I was stuck in the middle of a really good book.
I feel like buying some icecream, a cone, instead.
I'd someone to collect at the airport.
My computer is broken and receives no email,
so I've called a technician who's not arrived yet
and he has, as they do, a list of excuses
as long as your arm or a week of Sundays. To be honest
there's no need for the hard copy or an office
or an appointment, not for this
but it might take something like an appointment
to get me out of this eternal kitchen,
where I relive the 1.1 earthquake
that made the walls shiver around
the domestic scene I've left behind,
things truth be told I could not really broach
even with Russ, barber, unlikely muse, as he applies
the steel, the little slow juts and nicks and trims
of the number 3, as we keep in our field of vision
the box in the corner with the transfer latest,
something continuing outside this deep freeze.

Tom French

GOOD DOG

His lungs attempted to draw their first breath again
as the blue medicine entered and flooded the brain.
'*One in ten do it,*' the vet said, '*and it puts the heart
across you.*' We accepted him back in the carpark

as a warm parcel, and opted to call the hole we'd dug
'*the grave*', for the children's sake. Dog daisies took
the bare look off the clay. With the last of his Bonios
they made crosses. Our eldest kept coming back to

the spot as if he knew more; our youngest wanted
to know if Snoopy would come back as a horse.
The sight of her at the kennel, looking in, checking,
then looking away, trying to believe her eyes,

caught me out. We told them what we'd done
was best for the dog – blind and mostly deaf and in pain,
with winter coming – and kept a little of the clay
his body displaced to fill in when the ribs collapsed.

It was strange to feel grateful to him for the gentle lesson
in being here he'd taught our children. For the instants
before he entered Nowhere, he was a pup again, doing
something he had never done before, feeling the strange air

on his fur wet with afterbirth, searching out his milky mother
with new eyes, taking the world, all the oxygen it had to offer,
in.

Tom French

My father extends to me, as he has to my sisters,
the two uneven 'o's of our household scissors
in the hopes that I might bring myself to trim
the strands at the back that prove beyond him.

He has knelt up and given his word to be good.
If he moves a muscle now there will be blood.
Thus we grow accustomed to address each other –
I, to the back of his head, he, facing the mirror.

Since we have said all there is to say of weather –
it broke, it held, it broke, it held, it broke, father –
and this is his last visit and he is going away

and I have drawn the line at eyebrows and nostrils,
I present him with the gift of an eyebrow pencil
with which, with a little flourish, he signs our name.

Tom Mathews

ONE FOR THE MASTER

The speaker being a Princeton co-ed, the word 'bad' is to be considered in the demotic
American sense: cool, sexually attractive

Odi et amo, ever since we met, and yet, Armagh *virumque cano*.
Grey, owlish, celtic, charming, a romantic
And once I heard him speak
And tried to spell
My way through his critiques
(His marking is perhaps a tad pedantic)
My knees were weak
And so I fell,
Bad about the Moy, grand, and Saville-Row clad,
Or bare as Cupid, he's so bad about the Moy.
I guess I'm stupid
All the daydreams that I've had about the boy
And when they put my author on the stage
He breaks a heart with each *New Yorker* page.
Though people call him a flâneur
He knows his shopping list from Schopenhauer, I'm sure
There's just a touch of Count de Sade about the boy.
If I'm 'An amadawn'
What do I care?
Look in the Bangor pawnshop of his heart
You'll find me there.
He reads from *Quoof* and gives that goofy grin
And poof! I'm Pangur Bán upon a hot tin roof again.
I'm glad I signed up for this discipline.
And though I know that it's absurd
To spend my evenings looking up his words
It's just that he's so bad about the Moy.

Tom Mathews

EXPERIENTIA

Who, looking at the cloud
Conceives the thunder's clamour,
Foresees the lightning hurled?
But shepherds learn the weather
As cobblers learn leather
As a child learns the world.

Who, looking at the egg
Conceives the peacock's feather,
The hundred eyes unfurled?
So you and I together
Each round the other curled
Begin to learn each other
As a child learns the world.

Andrew Elliott

HENS

There are women in the East End of Glasgow
who wear their hair as short as the men to whom they are married.
It's an example of something they hold in common
with the women of East Berlin

with one of whom I found myself sharing a bed, back in 1987
and not just a bed but a joint and a joke about how,
had her husband seen us then he'd have taken us
by the throats and throttling us, carried us, kicking to the window

with its view of West Berlin, the border with its watchtowers
and the free world beyond, then worked the lock
with his teeth and tongue, butted it open with a *hieb* of his *heid*
and dangled us out in the thin air like a pair of hens bred for the
    broiler

which he'd only just pulled from the battery and from which he was
    shaking
the muck off. Yet being the man he was – a brute but fundamentally
decent – he would have baulked at letting go, tossing us
quivering back into our pit then, the lift being out, howling obscenities

over his shoulder, a red mist descending twenty-four flights of
    stairwell.
Not that we'd have missed for the world the sight of him crossing
the play park, stopping to look up when he got to his Trabant
and, seeing us shoulder to shoulder, shake his fist like a toy town
    commissar

then drive away and leave us, staring at what we weren't to know then
was the future until, covered in pimples, we ran back to bed,
took each other by the throat and lay there laughing uncontrollably
at the way our faces struck each other and how we couldn't get the
    words out.

Andrew Elliott

MIDDLE MAN

I am like the kind of man who took his own life
by the scruff of the neck and, afraid of the scene
it might make in the elevator, rushed it through
the marble lobby to where the stairwell started
and life, as he'd suspected, began to make things
difficult like a child resisting, banister by banister,
forcing him to fight it, flight by flight by flight
until, just short of the fiftieth floor, his intention
to show it the view from the top has all but been
overtaken by the feeling that he's not going to get there
which prompts him to curl up in a corner, let life go
and lie there listening for the crash of the fire door
back to the street to reach him and so know
that life has left the building and is out there doing
as it pleases, only to find that the longer he listens
the longer life is taking and, in the end, hears nothing.

Zoë Brigley

THE SCENT BOTTLE

'...the vessel in which she had sent my box, being stranded on the coast of Devonshire,
in consequence of which the box was dashed to pieces with the violence of the sea
and all my little property, with the exception of a very few articles, swallowed up in
the mighty deep.'
        – Maria Branwell, mother of the Brontë sisters, in a letter to her
            future husband, Patrick Brontë

It is a long time coming but when it does arrive,
it sits by the mirror, the glass body protruding
a severed stalk, silver eye, squat key.

I sit before it as if waiting for something
and cradle the shock of its cold body in my palm.
It is not as beautiful as when it was new

– blasted by salt and scratched by sailors –
and yet, in the deep heady scent of it
is something else: an ocean voyage skimming

the North Sea and rounding the coast for Penzance
to the blink of a teasing lighthouse,
the long beckoning of a weathered stone pier,

the slap of pilchards on the cobbles, and coracles
dwarfed by larger vessels: the *Amity* and *Fame*,
the *Grace*, the *One and All* and the *Happy Return.*

In its perfume is not only a wilderness of roses,
but the watery stench of the tide-waiter and mariner,
the pasteboard smell of printers and bookbinders,

the sickly maltsters on Market Jew Street
and the burnt liquorice of the tanners and saddlers,
the tang of the physician's, the caramel of boot-makers,

the foggy wool of the tailors and drapers,
the peruke maker's flowery chamber
and honeyed fat of the tallow-chandler,

grasping soot in the deepening shaft of Wherry Mine
and smelted tin, rasping metallic like blood on the tongue,
until the cork fits it again and that other place sets sail.

We wait together, the bottle and I, in the garden
where a patchwork moor spreads out before us
like a rough and mothering ocean and I stumble

out into the heather catching another scent on the wind.

Note: *tide-waiter*: customs official; *maltster*: maker of malt; *peruke maker*: wig
maker; *tallow-chandler*: a maker of candles from the suet or fat of animals.

Gary Allen

LINES

Those were the days of long queues
outside the dole offices
cardboard-stuffed shoes letting in rain
the pain of waiting like a sun that never shines
a piece of paper with numbers stamped on it
a piece of paper with your name stamped on it
a cigarette made of tobacco dust
as we did the dole queue shuffle, and waited
without speaking
without hope
without breakfast
and the man at the desk is angry with so much failure
tells us we are to blame
there is plenty of work out there
not the lame schools
or the engrained culture of the loser
or the bleeding state
as we each think like a chain
linked to a string of thoughts
like rain on telegraph-wires
and each of us thinks our own escape
each of us dreams a way out.

Everything is broken
the legs on the table in the kitchen
the rings on the cooker don't work
have burned out long ago
the toilet no longer flushes
bring out buckets of cold water
work a few hours in the slaughterhouse
for a parcel of cheap cuts
hands slashed like pieces of meat
all the time insane going round and round
on feet of water in the same direction
keeping stumm with one another
for who knows who will tell
who will succumb to the luxury of deceit.

Cider is cheap, like sex in an empty flat
where hardboard doors have been punched open
whose oil-cloth has been burned for heat
whose rooms echo with desperate voices
the smell of mince and onions in cheap boarding-houses
listen, I will be someone, we will be someone
this one will write a novel
this one will get an interview
she will win the lottery
she will go on the game for a half of whiskey
this one will O.D. in heaven with a smile
these two will find love among the washing-lines
this one will find poems in their dead voices
as the cider runs out
as the queue snakes quietly out of sight.

Kathy Mac

A PORTRAIT ARTIST'S DISAVOWED DESIRE

"I'm not a plastic surgeon," he asserts
to one disgruntled husband, and later
explains over a pint: "I paint what I see."

The palette knife only mixes colour,
never touches canvas. So he doesn't see
how he flays every woman he paints.

Kathy Mac

REVERSE OSCAR

" ... but most of all, and though I know
we should act as if we're
ultimately self responsible, and
though it's no longer fashionable

I'd like to blame
my mother

whose example taught me
not to trust, but to be
fruitlessly independent;

to work hard, to give it all
to projects that could never lead
to my heart's desire,

(because failure is so much less painful
when, deep down, you don't really care)

so there was no reason to figure out
where my heart's desire might lie;

to aim low;

and above all, to avoid disappointment
by expecting disappointment."

Nick Laird

INNER FLAP COPY

They like to start by saying poetry is nothing,
or there is nothing but, or poetry is nothing
but her mood, work done by the soul's hands
or tragicomic self-abuse, a dragnet raised
and emptied of three stickleback and four
grey pebbles, what I thought first, second,
fifth, such hardihood and trick-or-treat and
spite, the vestiges of sympathetic magic
or a pimped-out souped-up pussy-magnet,
vatic good or finest management of brand,
companionless nocturnal mammals' eldritch
calls or a series of temples raised to pretexts,
horripilated rapture in the motion crutches
give but profitless, a piece of shit, Elysium ...
Poetry I found you mooching out the back in
the loading bay at the meat factory, smoking
a rollie and eyeing the maggots writhing below
like disco rice on the ribbed concrete where
the crates are dropped by me, my ilk; or in
the softest smell of my wife's neck; or where
oddment clouds are lit from under at 4 p.m.
this Wednesday, as if dipped in molten gold
and flown like flags of no country a human
may set foot in, yet, and if I do suppose you
poetry to be our flawed compensation for
having just the one go, that does for me.

Nick Laird

ANNALS OF ALAN

My carrel on the eighth floor of lower Manhattan has a lot
of graffiti devoted to Alan. **Alan has the best weed.**
Alan is a woman. The walrus is Alan. Do we still need Alan?
Alan I want to have your baby. Alan taped my nana.
Fuck Obama Alan for president.

Alan is Geraldo Rivera. The victory is Alan's.
I hate being Alan. Alan is a dream most likely.
Who the heck is Alan? Alan is homosexy.
Alan is a social construct. *I love Alan.*
It all comes down to Alan. I AM ALAN.

Alan is over. **WE ARE ALL ALAN**. Remember when
there was no Alan? If I am so beautiful and if you love me so
much then spell my fucking name correctly –
ALLEN. No, it's Allan. No, it's Alain.
Alain, Alain, t'es beau et je t'aime.

Lauren Norton

Got a taste of the old fear
when the mounted police
clopped down Dawson Street,
of an eyeball torn from its gaze,
or some other loss –
the chocolate hands
stood on their own lopped
wrists for sale on carts in Belgium.

Painted students were rushing by the horses,
as large, inapt, as dinosaurs,
and the cars were patient as crocodiles.
There were still some pensioners
rattling about since their morning hurrah
outside the Dáil,
where they croaked for blood
and medical cards, resurrected Dev
and that other beaked thief
who gave them transit *gratis*.

Found the bike where I left it,
its spokes stuffed
with socialist pamphlets that broke
the quiet ticking
wheeling down Kildare Street.
A hundred keepers of the peace
milled outside the library
and the riot squad wore darker motley,
twisting their batons.

Donna Sørensen

THE PILGRIMAGE

The light rain, colour of fish-tears,
over Mitaka and hanging in the bare
blossom trees of Inokashira Park,
gently discouraged the worshipping hoards,
whispered droplets in their hair
and on their faces, pushing them back
to the blazing billboard temples;
the endless shopping malls.

It kept them in their high hotels,
lolling unsteadily over Tokyo
on tip-toe foundations, to gaze
out past their own reflections,
counting how many times
the city touched the sky.

Back down on earth, hidden beneath
my sagging black umbrella,
I entered the gateway alone
and crossed into his sacred world
of forest spirits, followed
silently down the museum's
low-lit corridors by masked wraiths,
plying me with gifts of gold.

I knew these ghosts; their promises.
I didn't need their trinkets.
I'd come for magic and found it,
staring out across a room full
of animators' secrets. Waiting
on a spinning zoetrope a little girl
held a skipping rope – she was not real.

My presence set a strobe in motion –
its slapping hand of light upon the girl
shocked her into life. She skipped
in front of me, eyes closed in smile,
alive for a magic minute
under Hayao Miyazaki's gaze.

Liam Carson

TIME IS THE KEY: 'TANGLED UP IN BLUE'

I believe in a God of space and time
– Bob Dylan

But the knot of causes in which I am entangled recurs and will create me again
– Friedrich Nietzsche

'I hate story songs', Dylan once declared, in a typical wind-up. 'Tangled Up in Blue' contains many stories. There's a story of a man running from his past, whilst trying to return to that same past. The narrator traverses the vast landscapes of America, in a breathless, hazy account of loves won and lost. The song explores space, time and identity. Dylan's 'I', his narrative voice, seems to belong to two different individuals. 'Tangled Up in Blue' is long, often taking ten minutes to perform on stage, but its musical and narrative drive never flags. It echoes Kerouac's vision of writing that 'went fast because the road is fast'.

Its composition marked a key point in Dylan's development. In the mid-Sixties Dylan heard a 'wild mercury sound': the songs poured through him, out of him, the muse came unbidden. Of *Highway 61 Revisited*, Dylan said, 'You can't sit down and write that consciously because it has to do with the break-up of time'.

Break-up of time lies at the heart of 'Tangled Up in Blue'. It is also a visual narrative. Dylan says, 'I wanted to defy time, so that the story took place in the present and past at the same time. When you look at a painting, you can see any part of it or see it all together. I wanted that song to be like a painting, to make the focus as strong as a magnifying glass under the sun'.

Early one morning, the sun was shining. In the first line, Dylan steps into the timeless world of traditional song.

> Early one morning, just as the sun was rising
> I heard a maid sing in the valley below

Dylan's teller wonders if his lover's 'hair was still red'. Perhaps it's the hennaed hair of a Sixties hippie girl. Perhaps it's a nod to 'Wildwood Flower':

> I will twine and I will mingle my weeping black hair
> With the roses so red and the lilies so fair

Is 'Tangled Up in Blue' autobiographical? Does it matter? Introducing the song in 1978, Dylan told audiences that 'it took ten years to live, and two years to write'. But we know Dylan did not work on a 'fishing boat right outside of Delacroix'. The song is about the Sixties. It's about a relationship or set of relationships that alter over time. Dylan's ambition in 'Tangled Up in Blue' is to create a narrative: 'You've got yesterday, today and tomorrow all in the same room, and there's very little that you can't imagine happening.' Like Kerouac speaking of the writing of *On the Road* in the poem 'Mexico City Blues' – 'make it a great story & confession / Of all the crazy people you've known / Since early Nineteen Fifty One' – Dylan compresses many events into a tight time-frame. 'I know every scene by heart, they all went by so fast', he sings on 'If you see her, say hello'.

'Imagine', perhaps, is the key word. The song belongs to the listener's imagination. This is something that Dylan always understood, that the singer is the vehicle for the song, not vice-versa. The singer is here to tell a tale. I listen to its swirl, imagine Dylan taking a deep breath before he plunges into the story. He tracks his lovers across America. I catapult myself into the cinema of my mind, let the days, the hours, the minutes flash by on the reels of the film. Moments in slow motion, moments in fast motion. I see myself in Mooreland Drive. I'm just sixteen. I lose myself in vast landscapes, places I've never seen – Delacroix, New Orleans, Montague Street. My parents are out, so I can play the singer. I stand before an invisible microphone, close my eyes. I see myself at the steering wheel, watching the country shacks and lonely railroad crossings race past the rain-lashed windscreen. I am both here and there.

On 8 July 1984, Dylan plays Slane Castle. I stand close to the front, this is my first Dylan gig. He's wiry, dressed in a long black overcoat, black jeans and biker boots, a zebra-patterned shirt; he's wearing face paint and mascara. Legs apart he stands still, centre-stage, the man at the centre of the vortex. His band churn out Sixties bar-room boogie blasted big, as they charge into 'Highway 61'. Eighty thousand fans fill the natural arena sweeping down to the waters of the Boyne. The sun still blazes, it's not dark yet, twilight begins. Bikers, Hell's Angels, punks, hippies, balding civil servants, students, all crushed together. Sweat rolls down my face, the crush lurches from side to side. It's getting harder to breathe. I need water. Four songs in, Dylan sings 'Just Like a Woman'. As he hits the line 'It was raining from the first / And I was dying there of thirst', the stage crew turn a water cannon on the audience. As one we cheer, relax, heads back, straining for the water from above.

During an acoustic set – Dylan and his guitar alone – he sings 'Tangled Up in Blue'. The pronouns shift around, the 'I' of the first three verses becomes 'He'. Verse five from the original is gone – the one with the 'Italian poet from the thirteenth century'. He is entranced by the woman 'working in the blinding light', not a 'topless place'; he tries to 'stay out of the joints'. The south is now as cold as the north.

We straggled away that night from the Dylan gig. I'd bumped into Anne, with whom I'd had a recent fling. In her bed-sit we listened to 'Jokerman' early in the morning. The night had fallen, and the road from the castle to the village was strewn with burnt-out cars from the drink-fuelled riots of the night before. Later we'd hear that one of Dublin's punk crew had drowned in the Boyne. Back in Dublin there were no jobs to be had, I was returning to sign on the dole and to stand in the street holding a sign for Freebird Records.

In *Chronicles*, Dylan says: 'I didn't know what age of history we were in nor what the truth of it was.' He postulates a cyclical view of time and history, one in which states and societies grow into maturity then collapse into decadence – where, in the words of the different versions of 'Tangled Up in Blue, 'finally the bottom fell out', or 'it all came crashing down'.

In the face of this erosion of his world, the storyteller has 'to keep on keepin' on'. He echoes Junior Walker's '(I'm a) Road Runner', which sang of a man in flight from all ties:

> All my life I've been like this
> If you love me, it's your own risk
> When the dust hits my shoes
> I got the urge to move
>
> Said, I'm a roadrunner, baby
> Just keep on, keepin' on

But he also echoes Curtis Mayfield's 'Keep on Keeping On', an elegy for the dreams of a time when 'revolution was in the air', with its valedictory conclusion:

> Many think that we have blown it
> But they too will soon admit
> That there's still a lot of love among us
>
> And there's still a lot of faith, warmth, and trust
> When we keep on keeping on

Thus emerge contradictory impulses, layers of potential meaning. 'Tangled Up in Blue' contains the poetry of pared down, demotic language. 'Early one morning', 'the axe just fell', 'something inside of him died'. It is the language of plain talk that is anything but plain. It is a whirlpool of song, poetry and history. When Dylan sings of the 'dark sad night', you can see the ghost of Woody Guthrie's Tom Joad taking 'flight in the dark rainy night'. Dylan's narrator has 'rain fallin' on my shoes'. In Kerouac's *The Subterraneans*, he speaks of rain '[kissing] everywhere men and women and cities in one wash of sad poetry'.

'Tangled Up in Blue' compresses space and time. One line that jolts the listener is, 'Then he started into dealing with slaves and something inside of him died', which begs the question of whether the slaves are purely metaphorical or have an actual historical presence. Interviewed by Lynne Allen in 1978, Dylan found the American Civil War echoed in his life. 'There was a network all across the country – really. Very small, but very close, I still see those people traveling around. They're still hanging in there. But as far as what happened, it will always be felt just the same as the Civil War was always felt into 1870 and 1880. It was just something which was felt by everyone whether they knew it or not and a lot of people in the Sixties started all this which is happening now.'

There may not be actual slaves in the story – they may be slaves in the sense that they are slaves to the system, to Mammon. They may be slaves to drugs. 'Dealing with slaves' might also hint at Rimbaud. But in the context of New Orleans and Delacroix, the word 'slaves' cannot help but evoke the realities of history.

And the 'blue' of the title? Is Blue a person, like the Baby Blue he once sang of? Blue is the entire universe of mood and memory attached to Dylan's characters. Dylan has mentioned that he wrote the song after immersing himself in Joni Mitchell's *Blue*. When Mitchell sings 'and a bar maid came by in fishnet stockings', you can imagine it might be in the same 'topless place' Dylan's narrator steps into.

Interviewed about his film *Renaldo and Clara*, Dylan pointed to its use of colour, notably 'cobalt blue'. In 'You're gonna make me lonesome when you go', Dylan mentions the northern town of Ashtabula on the coast of Lake Erie. In *Chronicles*, he pays homage to Carl Sandburg, 'the poet of the prairie and the city'. Sandburg's 'Crossing Ohio When Poppies Bloom in Ashtabula' sings of 'light blue kites on a deep blue sky'. Blue is also the open space of America. In *Blue Highways: A Journey into America*, William Least Heat Moon writes:

> On the old highway maps of America, the main routes were red and the back roads blue. Now even the colors are changing. But in those brevities just before dawn and a little after dusk – times neither day nor night – the old roads return to the sky some of its color. Then, in truth, they carry a mysterious cast of blue, and it's that time when the pull of the blue highways is strongest...

Sometimes the narrator's journey has no plan, he 'drifts' down to New Orleans, just as a later song declares 'people don't live or die, people just float'. And so the vast majority of my friends hit the boat for England at the tail end of that summer of 1984. We drift over in two and threes, and the tide swells and swells. We follow the tide of human events.

In our last summer in Dublin, friends Trish, Dermot and I roamed the city together, prowling the bars of a Saturday night. The Pygmalion. Bartley Dunne's. Searching for parties, gigs. We'd dance at the Afro Spot or the Hirschfield Centre in Temple Bar. Trish and I shared a flat with another friend Gary MacMahon – 9 South Circular Road was a former brothel, we found out.

Dermot, Trish and I formed what we saw as a gestalt. The idea came from Theodore Sturgeon's science fiction novel, *More than Human*. In it, a group of misfit or disturbed individuals – including Gerry, an enraged street urchin and Janie, a telepathic child – come together to create a gestalt, a single being that together is whole, more than the sum of its parts. Such a thing, of course, could not last. We were fired by destiny, and magic. Consulting the *I Ching* and the Tarot. We wrote and shared short stories and poems. We read Colin Wilson's *The Outsider* and Carl Jung's *Memories, Dreams and Reflections*.

'Tangled Up In Blue' takes us in every direction of the compass. The singer '[heads] out for the East Coast'; gets 'a job in the Great North Woods', abandons a car 'out West'; then heads south to New Orleans. It's worth noting that in certain occult systems, the compass points have the following divinatory meanings – east/future; west/past; north/possibility; and south/present.

By autumn 1984 we are in London. Dermot and Trish get a flat together; my ex-girlfriend Marjorie says I can crash in her Brixton squat for a while. We end up seeing each other again. It freezes that winter, we go to bed with layers of clothes, a single-bar heater hisses and crackles through the night. There's no hot water. In the mornings, a kettle is boiled for a shave.

> There was snow all winter and no heat
> Revolution was in the air

'Tangled Up in Blue' contains ghosts and echoes of earlier Dylan songs. 'We just saw it from a different point of view' reprises 'One Too Many Mornings' and its assertion that 'you're right from your side, I'm right from mine'. In 'Bob Dylan's Dream', friends are 'never seen again'; he evokes young idealists never imagining 'that the one road we travelled would ever shatter and split'. In 1984's 'Tangled up in Blue' he sang 'one day he could just feel the waste, he put it all down and split'.

By 1987 I was in my last squat in London – 44 Oval Mansions. Ian Dury used to live there, and my bedroom was covered with Blockheads stickers. The Band of Holy Joy lived in New Cross Gate, but spent much of their time in the Mansions. I'd knock back pints with their singer Johnny Brown in The Royal Oak. Their first album *Tales from the City* boasted big sea-shanty melodies built on mad waltz tempos. They played violins, old-style synthesizers, accordions, trumpets and banjos; theirs was a big, lush, sound. The songs inhabited an inner city universe not far removed from that of The Pogues. Johnny loved street-banter, wordplay, folk yarns, urban myths, William Burroughs, anything weird, off-kilter, and disturbing. Junkies, fishwives, child kidnappers, beggars, thieves, fairies and whores prowled a landscape of broken glass, pubs, canals, backstreets and decaying flats. Here were domestic violence, drunken babies, kids drinking cider in the park, rendered in hypnotic, hallucinatory lyrics. It was the world that lay about us, and in us. Friends flirted with smack, became slaves to it. One day our squat was broken into, and Dermot's money nicked. I suggested a mutual friend who had fast become a junkie was probably responsible. Her goldfish had begun to eat each other. I could smell the tail of the dragon everywhere. Dermot and I had a fight, and the next morning I began packing.

I put it all down and split London. Wondering what the hell I had done, stunned in my skin. I returned to Belfast, a dark city I no longer knew, where most of my world had vanished. There was just Mart, Mitch and I meeting to slag each other on a Saturday night. I'd stagger out of Maddens Bar, shouting a line from 'Señor':

> This place don't make sense to me no more

At the end of 'Tangled up in Blue', the narrator realises 'I got to get back to her somehow', whilst simultaneously admitting he is 'heading for another joint'. Is he returning or continuing? Is he doing both? Kerouac wrote of his travels, 'Here I was at the end of America…no more land…and nowhere was nowhere to go but back'. The journey, the story starts over. Nietzsche's 'entangled…knot of causes' begins again.

There is 1978's version. There are no drums. It is now a torch ballad, Dylan's emotionally charged grand singing entwined with saxophone and piano. It is intimate. One could believe Dylan was telling his own story here.

> All the people we used to know
> They're an illusion to me now
> Some are mathematicians
> Some are carpenters' wives
> Don't know how it all got started
> I don't know what they're doing with their lives

'Time is the key' sang Patti Smith. Dylan, who will turn seventy on 24 May, is increasingly preoccupied with time – 'The end of time has just begun'; 'time is running away'; and with forgetfulness – 'forgetful heart / lost your power of recall / every little detail / you don't remember at all'; and with loss – 'when you think that you've lost everything / you find out you can always lose a little more'. But even on the unreleased *Blood on the Tracks* song 'Up to Me', Dylan sang: 'Death kept followin', trackin' us down, at least I heard your bluebird sing / Now somebody's got to show their hand, time is an enemy'. And in using the phrase 'time out of mind' as an album title, Dylan clearly refers to a time that is beyond memory, slipping into oblivion.

1997. I am walking in Temple Bar on a morning where the sun has broken through the clouds, steam rises from the cobblestones. From a distance of ten yards or so, a woman catches my eye. It's someone I know, but for the life of me, I just can't place her. She smiles as I pass, and I smile back. I turn to look at her as she is walking away, and she looks over her shoulder. For hours after, I rifle through the files of my memory, tease out the tangled connections. Finally it comes to me. Helen. We were at college together, in the same English class. But time and space have taken us far from the world of thirteen years ago. It's all an illusion to me now.

If ever there was an artist who defines himself in terms of the road, or the concept of the road, it is Dylan. On 'Up to Me', he warns those for whom 'life is a pantomime' that they 'don't have all that much time'. He goes on to say 'One of us has got to hit that road, I guess it must be up to me'.

There's a blurred film of a 2006 live version of 'Tangled Up In Blue', taken at speed, close to the patterns of the original. Dylan is on a stage decorated with a huge compass. At one of its points he stands crouched over his electric piano, legs shuffling, kicking; he bends into the piano. He claps his hands. His voice shifts from a high yelp to a low growl on alternate lines, every syllable hits the beat. The energy crackles, the riff goes round and round, the circle, the vortex of time spins. Dylan's 'long and lonesome' artistic road takes him to 'the last outback at the world's end'. Like Beckett, he can't go on, but he will go on.

Listen again. The song contains multitudes. The story is being told again, only this time it is different. What was once present is now the past. Once more it's up to the poet to drag the past out into the light.

> Me, I'm still on the road
> Headed for another joint
> We always did feel the same
> We just saw it from a different point of view
> Tangled up in blue

Sean Borodale

from BEE JOURNAL

29 September

Archangel sun
  held to a flower's remnant
a weighing of balance in the sway of asters
I saw two days before
  as though the angled plane
of the flat face of September's sun
  had made each flower's inflorescence
    mirror its gift
We are inflected. Note:
  Bees give by this

Sean Borodale

from BEE JOURNAL

7 October: Wasps

Torrents of wasp – five at once, fifty, erratic, persistent
Bee peace is bombed at this house. But
distortion in their world is articulate
The air's single cell is clear as a bauble, and delicate
They know the invertebrate bubble of the planet's life-jacket
and do sustain it – this weird filigree of livid minute

It seems mirage to us; sceptical ill-tuned folk
bees heatwave off the hive's wooden mouth
As for wasps, it's like
short sparks which jump from loose plug leads
into an engine's block

Today then, I watched a threading of loose ends

Sean Borodale

from BEE JOURNAL

11 October: Michaelmas Daisies

Bright day, afternoon, no precise time
the hour-light at sunlight's maximum
Michaelmas daisies are set to now

Alight honey bee
                    I do feel
the extremity of your spectrum
that homes on an unsteady cymbal of flower's radial
I heard it shivering tissh as you touched on its platform
a close-up protracting of tongue suck in a zip-noise
a faint sweet wet from a nectary's spring

We observe the yellowness of dying leaves
it's like gates it's like precincts being drawn
to 3D's infinity point of perspective
The shawl-work of summer has grown unwoven
tuned into a brittle, rottable music of roughage and stubborn dregs

The earth-she wanders, going blind and odd
like air pushing a trolley, full of dead flowers

is that not you, Persephone, or Eurydice, or just a likeness
creeping

Listen,
        small pitch patch of bee wing song
is strung with a sound made of now's last flowerheads

Maybe just
our time ticks because we have a time to accord to
And all the machinery is lifted by briefest experience
Echoes are something more quiet
than a world's bee paused on a ledge, at an edge
for a life of a few weeks
cycling up from millennia's blackness

We are played in your existence
and the Shadows we bring
fall just a note's breadth
off your heart-rate's strumming

Sean Borodale

from BEE JOURNAL

17 October: Super Check

Removed the Honey Super

No stores, just a dry papery wax-comb of empties
No sugar syrup touched. What is wrong with supplements?

Stand mesmerised at this landing board. It is familiar,
all-relevant, a collateral winding of wire-string song

Think what paths would be if we could envisage
flights tracked to their nectaries pin-point co-ordinates
A round dance tells trails
in mid-air's mile or so round-trip

We bring, bee friend, yellow pollen on our legs

In human terms, it seems OK
Your bright sharp blackthorn-rickety bodies pass each way

I lay a minute's judgment. Minute, small
                              Perhaps a touch
vacant, a field-slack lethargy. Something I dreamt
still nameless is coagulating its weak-spot under our nose

Burdock burrs gather and catch on our gauze as we hack
the thicket clear of the hive for winter air to not stagnate

We suffer damp, dear neighbour – you should not

Seán Lysaght

WHAT IS ECO-POETRY?

In 1889, as W B Yeats surveyed the image of nature in ancient folklore, he declared, 'Once every people in the world believed that trees were divine, and could take a human or grotesque shape and dance among the shadows of the woods; and deer, and ravens and foxes, and wolves and bears, and clouds and pools, almost all things under the sun and moon, and the sun and moon, not less divine and changeable: they saw in the rainbow the still bent bow of a god thrown down in his negligence; they heard in the thunder the sound of his beaten water-jar, or the tumult of his chariot wheels; and when a sudden flight of wild duck, or of crows, passed over their heads, they thought they were gazing at the dead hastening to their rest'.

The passage reminds us of the antiquity of our symbolic practice through the natural world and how, in the early stages of culture, the relationship with nature was instinctual; it was untroubled by the aesthetic and political categories that intrude on our own attempts at capturing the world around us. Throughout the modern period in art and literature, artists have been fascinated by the primal simplicity of ancient representations and a new value has been given to these primitive forms. For artists as diverse as D H Lawrence, Pablo Picasso, and the French and German Expressionists, the naïve power of primitive art was exemplary. The rough, impulsive lines of modern sculpture are only intelligible if we set them beside the primitive totems and icons that inspired them.

One of the qualities that adds to the mystique of primitive forms is their silence: they come down to us from cultures that did not have writing, so there is usually no parallel narrative to explain them. Our literature, by comparison, is complex; it can celebrate – as Yeats did – the early magical relationship with nature, but it will usually do so from the distance of its own situation in the modern world. Such was the case of D H Lawrence, for all his advocacy of primal energy.

If modern artists, including poets, have felt the need to articulate the relationship with nature programmatically, it is because of the felt distance between our culture and the natural manifold. Over the centuries, many factors have conditioned our human alienation from nature, including the iconography of medieval Christianity, the abstractions of Puritanism and of classicism, and, latterly, the modern industrial world. One of the key influences, which has punctured that alienation, has been the rediscovery of folk tradition: we find it in the green world, as celebrated in Shakespeare's comedies *As You Like It* and *A Midsummernight's Dream*, in the folk sources of romantic art, and in the miscellanies and tales of Celtic revivals.

Given the antiquity of our habits in this regard, and given thousands of years of symbolic practice, is there anything new in the notion of *eco-poetry*? Our age has certainly increased the stresses on the natural world, and brought environmental issues to the heart of our politics, but the call for a reverent attitude to nature has many precedents, especially in romantic poetry: Blake's *Songs of Innocence and Experience* (1794) shows an Edenic pastoral world being destroyed by industry and warfare, while Wordsworth's *Excursion* (1814) contains an impassioned plea for protection of the rural landscape from the spread of industry. We know that environmental issues bear on our politics with acute urgency, but what of their impact on poetry? I'd like to look at two Irish instances of writing to approach this question; these are the collections published by Derek Mahon since the turn of the century, and John F Deane's major statement of the question from a religious viewpoint in his recent book, *The Works of Love: Incarnation, Ecology and Poetry* (Columba, 2010).

In his 2005 collection, *Harbour Lights*, Derek Mahon published a substantial manifesto-poem called 'Resistance Days' in which he renewed his connection with the bohemian modernism of the Twentieth century. He specifically announces a return to 'creative anarchy', 'not the faux anarchy of media culture / but the real chaos of indifferent nature'. This anarchy in the cosmos serves Mahon as a kind of primal disorder to which we will all eventually return and from which both our consciousness and our art spring. The process is analysed in another poem from the same book, 'The Cloud Ceiling' where, as a young baby grows in her awareness of the world, the poet wonders about the emergence of thought:

> Are thoughts a tap trickle, a cloud formation?
> Given to light readings and rich inactivity,
> alternative galaxies, a-tonal composition
> and tentative revisions of quantum gravity,
> you drift in a universe of unspoken words
> far from the bright lights and story-boards.

If this ecology of awareness is informed by modern cosmic physics, there are other moments where Mahon refers explicitly to biological science. In the title poem, 'Harbour Lights', the poet envisions human experience as a function of all life, especially its original and originating marine form. A day in the poet's consciousness is ending – as his own life approaches its late phase – and as it does so he looks forward to new beginnings:

dim souls wriggle in seething chaos, body
language and new thought forming there already
in hidden depths and exposed rock oases,
those secret cultures where the sky pauses

One of the strengths of this idea in Mahon, beyond its objective foundation
in the story of evolution, is that it can operate as a process of consolidation,
of life, myth, or art, or as a process of dispersal, of the end of a human
life, or of a whole civilisation. In its most recent versions, Mahon's doctrine
of the world has absorbed Hindu influences and keeps underlining rebirth,
reincarnation and an endless process of re-invention. Nothing is ever lost
in this formulation; as one order passes away, the elements are there for
its renewal:

Enough, already, with the failed
agendas; give the Algonquin back
the shiny vein of ore we struck
and watch them re-enchant the world!
— 'BLUEPRINT'

In the 2008 collection, *Life on Earth*, Mahon's references to the environment
and to science are advertised more explicitly. The title itself signals the
influence of David Attenborough, while a key sequence in the book,
'Homage to Gaia', holds a door open to James Lovelock's theories of the
earth's ecosystem and to debates about global warming. The title poem
of the 'Homage to Gaia' sequence offers an apology 'to you, / great Gaia
our first mother / with your confused retinue / of birds, your weird
weather.'

The idiom of this collection, and of Mahon's recent work generally, is
eclectic: references to science and to the excesses of modern capitalism
('dirty tricks and genocidal mischief') sit comfortably with his older
Ovidian and existential themes. The mandarin poet, who has 'read all the
books', can now spin out his prolix discourse on the widest range of
experience, and is not averse to anything – he can even consider
supermarket music ('ambient retail rock') before dismissing it. When you
consider this cosmopolitan ease, along with its formal accomplishments,
there is something not quite convincing about Mahon's espousal of 'the
real chaos of indifferent nature' ('Resistance Days'). As if aware of this
tension himself, he has tried, in 'A Quiet Spot' from *An Autumn Wind*
(2010), to clear out all the encumbrances of his cosmopolitan culture and
focus on his Irish retreat in Kinsale. 'Gaia demands your love,' he insists
'the patient earth / your airy sneakers tread expects / humility and care.'

This in itself is a rhetorical flourish, to be set beside many others
throughout these recent collections. At these moments the 'eco-poetry'

is simply an extension of other discourses, where the well-informed, socially competent (in German: *salonfähig*) poet gossips about his fashionable neighbourhood:

A world of dikes and bikes
  where yoghurt-weavers drive
on gin and margarine...
  This is how to live

in the post-petroleum age...

Or, less ironically, but still with unruffled ease, Mahon declares in a recent poem, 'Dreams of a Summer Night' (2010),

So many quiet shores 'bleared, smeared with toil',
there's nowhere for a sticky duck to hide
from the unchecked invasion of crude oil
dumped on the sand by a once friendly tide;
and if they drill here what else do we gain
but a bonanza for an acquisitive crowd
of blow-hard types, determined, garish, loud?

Mahon's imaginative ecology is a facet of a wider set of accomplishments, which he exercises with relish in this late stage in his career. This reflex carries with it and comprehends his familiar genius for myth, for founding creative perception in lost, abandoned objects of our civilisation; in its radical political aspect Mahon's eco-poetry renews an older, mid-century bohemianism with surprising success – all this in a literary idiom of consummate control.

This connection with the natural world and the wider cosmos takes its cue from modern science. While not averse to transcendent values, which its ironic reach can capture at will, Mahon's recent poetry is firmly positioned in this world. As he puts it in 'Homage to Goa',

Given a choice of worlds, here or beyond,
I'd pick this one not once but many times
whether as mozzie, monkey or pure mind.

In a very different way, ecology is headlined by John F Deane in his recent biographia literaria, *The Works of Love: Incarnation, Ecology and Poetry* (2010). Deane's approach to the modern problem of environmental degradation is from the perspective of a deeply-held, learned Christianity. His environmental concern is summed up by the American writer Thomas

Berry, whom he quotes late in the book: 'To learn how to live graciously together would make us worthy of this unique, beautiful, blue planet that evolved in its present splendour over some billions of years, a planet that we should give over to our children with the assurance that this great community of the living will lavish on them the care that it has bestowed so abundantly upon themselves.' There are many aspects to this ambitious book that fall outside the scope of this article; for present purposes I'd like to look at how the author presents a large-scale matrix of Christian doctrine and poetic practice to underpin his love of nature as landscape and creation.

Deane grounds his belief in several doctrinal points: firstly, he restates the covenant of the Old Testament, which God made with Noah after the flood, 'with you and your descendants after you and with every living creature that was with you – the birds, the livestock and all the wild animals, all those that came out of the ark with you – every living creature on earth' (Genesis 9: 8-10). This idea of the covenant between God and Man gets extended in the New Testament by a number of ideas, principally the identification of God with his creation through the Incarnation, where the gap between transcendence and immanence is bridged, and by the Eucharist, where humanity partakes of the divine substance. One of the most elegant statements of this view of creation is a paraphrase of Simone Weil, on page 381:

> Weil held that the whole of creation is subject to the forward-urging power of God's love, which she terms 'necessity', the engine as it were driving the whole creation onward, through its seasons, its births, its deaths, its growth; she also sees this as 'obedience', the whole of the natural world being true to its created nature, and the radiance of this obedience, when humanity grows aware of it, we see as beauty.

Although Deane musters a wide array of writers to make his Christian and ecological beliefs cohere, he is still faced with the reality that 'there has been an utter dichotomy between human behaviour in its effort at "progress" and the well-being of the planet on which this progress was to have occurred' (p. 352). In his chapter on the American writer Wendell Berry, he also surveys modern statements from the Vatican and finds that the Catholic Church has been wanting in its support for the planetary cause. For example, a papal encyclical of 2009, *Caritas in Veritate*, drew the following comment from Donal Dorr in *The Furrow* (quoted in Deane, p. 353): 'I think it is a pity that Benedict, who is so committed on environmental issues, did not locate everything he has to say about business activity in this time of economic crisis within the broader context of the ecological crisis of our time.' At this point, and later when he confronts the reality of warfare and persecution, the search for a coherent doctrine stumbles over the crux of modern excesses, what Mahon calls 'the dirty tricks and genocidal mischief' of capitalism. In this respect, Deane's tenacity as a witness of what he calls 'works of love' – in art, literature, and human kindness generally – supersedes his attempts at giving his environmentalism a kind of doctrinal authority.

As part of this witness, he takes us through a survey of English poets to show how their love of nature was infused with religious belief. He suggests that the poetry of Henry Vaughan (1621–1695) was 'the first time in poetry in English that God, creation and human beings, the movement of the soul and the movement of the earth and heavens, all come together in a unified vision' (pp. 169-70). Over a century later, John Clare would again represent this religious faith in wild and rural nature as the signature of God. As Clare wrote in 'The Eternity of Nature':

> Leaves from eternity are simple things
> To the world's gaze – whereto a spirit clings
> Sublime and lasting – trampled underfoot
> The daisy lives and strikes its little root
> Into the lap of time – centurys may come
> And pass away into the silent tomb
> And still the child hid in the womb of time
> Shall smile and pluck them when this simple rhyme
> Shall be forgotten like a churchyard-stone

As is well-known, Clare brought an unusually detailed knowledge of wildlife and the landscape to his work from the perspective of the agricultural labourer. His work is also textured with many dialect words and irregularities of spelling in the manuscripts. Deane shows us how this grounded vision was shaped and given coherence by religious faith. 'His faith,' writes Deane, 'continues unquestioning, even in the depths of his wrecking and being wrecked' (p. 251). Throughout his later years of confinement in the Northampton Asylum, Clare continued to affirm his nature creed in terms like these:

> I love the haunts of solitude
> The coverts of the free
> Where man ne'er ventures to intrude
> And God gives peace to me.

Another, central chapter in *The Works of Love* is devoted to Gerard Manley Hopkins, whom Deane discovered shortly after the death of his wife Barbara. 'I immersed myself in it,' he writes. 'It moved me with

such power that I spent an entire night sitting at the kitchen table until
the dawn light was already greying the window' (p. 265). Hopkins is a key
example for Deane of a religious poet who plots an intense Christian
faith through praise and worship of the natural world. Hopkins's
relishing of nature's details was constant evidence for the witness of his
faith. At the end of 'Pied Beauty', following its catalogue of celebration,
Hopkins declares, 'He fathers-forth whose beauty is past change: / Praise
him.' Again and again in Hopkins's work we are drawn into a rush of
ecstasy at the beauty of creation, 'Because the Holy Ghost over the bent /
World broods with warm breast and with ah! bright wings' ('God's
Grandeur'). Summing up these encounters with the divine through love
of the creation, Deane writes, 'There is no doubt that his love of beauty,
of the physical things and patterns of the world, took on more than a
sacramental force for him.' As a further extension of this idea, he explains
that as a Christian committed to the Eucharist, Hopkins also needs 'to
know … Christ in his creation, in the wonder and awe and indeed in the
pain that nature herself endures' (p.268).

Hopkins does, however, occasionally write about nature without
drawing out or drawing down this sacramental value. In the poem
'Inversnaid', about a mountain brook that Hopkins saw on a visit to
Scotland in September 1881, the poet's focus is entirely on the object:

> This darksome burn, horseback brown,
> His rollrock highroad roaring down,
> In coop and in comb the fleece of his foam
> Flutes and low to the lake falls home.
>
> A windpuff-bonnet of fawn-froth
> Turns and twindles over the broth
> Of a pool so pitchblack, fell-frowning,
> It rounds and rounds Despair to drowning.

Although this poem portrays wild nature in a threatening aspect, its
beauty is undiminished. The pools of such mountain streams are
forbidding, yet fascinating, a quality that the romantics referred to as the
sublime. With the line 'It rounds and rounds Despair to drowning', I feel
that Hopkins gives rein to a darker response to the wild landscape, where
our humanity feels denied or alienated: the feeling evoked by the rushing
brook in its mountain setting is destructive, a function of the hostility of
the wild world. Therefore I cannot agree with Deane's reading of this
line, as he says that the burn was 'a place where despair itself, faced with
such beauty, must vanish' (p. 283). Instead, I feel that the drowning of
despair in the river's spate is the annihilation of all human feeling, of all
analogy to our world and its preoccupations. Be that as it may, Hopkins

still asserts that this raw world, with its appeal as well as its repulsion, is one that we continue to be drawn to:

> What would the world be, once bereft
> Of wet and of wildness? Let them be left,
> O let them be left, wildness and wet;
> Long live the weeds and the wilderness yet.

In summary, both Mahon and Deane situate their ecology, and their poetry of that ecology, within broader contexts. In the case of Mahon, his eco-poetry is coloured with the prestige of modern science as well as with antecedents in classical literature. In the case of Deane, 'ecology' is a theoretical term to give point to his real, and persuasive love of the natural environment, especially the landscape of his native Achill. *The Works of Love* includes a piece about 'The Meadows of Asphodel' on Achill:

> Bog cotton flourishes on the wild acres of bog on Achill Island. The thin
> stems offer a fine and woolly head of white that blows gallantly in the
> sea winds. Here and there amongst the cottons you will find the fine
> yellow heads of bog asphodel. Asphodel, according to the great stories
> of our mythology, is beloved of the dead and covers the plains of Hades.
> I came to have a vision of the surface of the bogs of Achill Island as
> imaging those rich and wind-blown plains of the afterworld, and the
> beautiful and delicate bog cotton plants stirring like a chorus of souls
> arrayed for paradise, prepared to utter into praise.

This image of the heads of bog cotton 'stirring like a chorus of souls arrayed for paradise' raises a question: can we assent to the beauty of this figuration without also assenting to the religious belief underlying it? (An image such as this, in its classical cast, would also be congenial to Mahon's poetic). Deane's answer to this question would, presumably, be no; and he enlists an impressive body of writers in support of his case, including Nicholas Boyle, Goethe's great modern biographer, whom I had not come across before as a religious writer. Deane quotes the Brazilian theologian Leonard Boff as follows: 'Beginning a new covenant with the earth absolutely requires a reclamation of the dimension of the sacred' (p. 411).

In aesthetic terms, particularly with regard to literature, this insistence is echoed by George Steiner's 1989 essay *Real Presences*. Steiner argues here that our Western tradition of high achievement in the arts is underpinned by religious belief, and that a belief in the mystery of transcendence sustains our systems of meaning. If this were true, then John F Deane's asphodels on Achill were unintelligible, in their wonderful aspect as a chorus of souls, to those of us who do not share religious sentiment, let alone belief.

The idea of real presence, which is normally an aspect of transubstantiation in the Eucharist, is enlisted by Steiner and applied to aesthetics generally, as well as to language in particular. The basic argument here is that language has an ability to communicate the world, that there is a covenant between the word and the world, and that this covenant is founded on belief in mystery and the transcendent. Where that belief declines, the covenant between language and the world breaks down and leads to the crisis of language in modernism. (This is a topic Steiner has reiterated many times, since the publication of *Language and Silence* in 1967).

These ideas are important in the present context because they clarify a central issue: the ability of language and poetry to communicate the world. This capacity of language haunted a writer such as Coleridge, who analysed it in his *Biographia Literaria* and defined it as *imagination*. The same focus is seen in Hopkins's inscape and instress, in Joyce's epiphanies, and in Heaney's famous formulation of 'that moment when the bird sings very close / To the music of what happens.' We have this revelatory power in Keats's 'gathering swallows', in Hopkins's 'pool so pitchblack, fell-frowning', and in John Clare, as he describes how 'Showers o'er the landscape fly on wet pearl wings'. We need go no further in order to locate 'eco-poetry': if ecology is the study of relationships between organisms in an environment, then poetry operates in that context simply by 'meaning' the world around us. It needs no further rationale from science, environmental politics, or indeed from religion to make its case. There are many extraordinary moments where poetry captures the natural environment; where these moments are addressed by a critical idiom they cannot be accounted for, only celebrated. Derek Walcott's white egrets and Dermot Healy's barnacle geese participate in this enigma. It is one for which academic commentary has no explanatory terminology, unless critical theory takes up an overtly hostile position with its jaded doctrines of 'the arbitrary nature of the linguistic sign' and 'inter-textuality'. And one final critical point: the unexplained power of language to capture and restore our experience of nature is something we can point to without resorting to sacred paradigm. 'We flinch,' writes Steiner, 'from the immediate pressures of mystery in poetic, in aesthetic acts of creation'. The mystery is entirely secular, and we encounter it every day, as Derek Mahon puts it at the conclusion of his recently published poem, 'Dreams of a Summer Night' (Gallery Press, 2010):

> I await the daylight we were born to love:
> birds at a window, boats on a rising wave,
> light dancing on dawn water, the lives we live.

Benjamin Keatinge

NEGOTIATING THE SECOND COLLECTION

Dave Lordan, *Invitation to a Sacrifice* (Salmon Poetry, 2010), €12.
Philip McDonagh, *The Song the Oriole Sang* (Dedalus Press, 2010), €12.50.
Ger Reidy, *Drifting Under the Moon* (Dedalus Press, 2010), €11.

Any poetry reviewer, faced with three volumes by emerging rather than
fully-established voices will seek overlaps and common ground, either by
way of themes or formal properties, through which to view the collections
under review. However, in the case of these three poets, there is little
enough poetic common ground on which to base such a contrastive
analysis. What we find instead is three poets whose second collections
extend the strengths of their first collections without calling for significant
re-evaluation of the poetic competencies and styles identified by their
first reviewers. Dave Lordan's performances of his own verse are well-
known to Irish audiences. Philip McDonagh is a diplomat whose postings
have taken him from London, to India to Rome and to Finland and most
recently Russia where he is currently Irish ambassador. Like Philip
McDonagh, Ger Reidy (born 1958) turned to poetry in his middle years
while continuing his professional work as a civil engineer in his native Co
Mayo. McDonagh and Reidy lean towards a well-crafted lyricism, albeit
with tonal and thematic differences. Lordan, on the other hand, uses a
powerful and torrential invective, after the manner of Allen Ginsberg, to
excoriate our political and social malaise as the post-Celtic Tiger
hangover really sets in.

Of course, Dave Lordan has already had a significant impact on the
Irish poetry scene since his first collection *The Boy in the Ring* (Salmon
Poetry, 2007), which won the Rupert and Eithne Strong award for Best
First Collection, and he remains as vibrant a performer as any on the
poetry circuit. The new collection *Invitation to a Sacrifice* confirms Lordan's
reputation as an outspoken, indeed, denunciatory voice against the political
establishment and the villains of Ireland's current economic plight.

However, strong opinions do not always translate into strong poems
and this collection is more markedly uneven as well as stylistically
heterodox than *The Boy in the Ring*. The first section of *Invitation to a
Sacrifice*, 'Surviving the Recession' exhibits the greatest formal assurance
with the outstanding 'Funeral City Passeggiata' coming closest to describing
the Valhalla or Styx of modern Dublin in a kind of steam-roller invective
which never gets out of control:

Nothing has ever happened here except us being dead.
It's a giant morgue with freezing empty theatres and cinemas,
a castellated tomb with a lake-sized moat,
an artificial island grave.
It's like we're miles beneath an invisible mountain inside an
   unreachable cave.
We bear it well. We're getting on all the same in our deaths.

Lordan's diagnostics of the recession have all the angry surrealism of Ginsberg's denunciations of his own 1950s malaise, in 'Howl', in which his contemporaries famously:

> ... were burned alive in their innocent flannel suits on Madison Avenue amid blasts of leaden verse & the tanked-up clatter of the iron regiments of fashion & the nitroglycerine shrieks of the fairies of advertising & the mustard gas of sinister intelligent editors, or were run down by the drunken taxicabs of Absolute Reality,

> who jumped off the Brooklyn Bridge this actually happened and walked away unknown and forgotten into the ghostly daze of Chinatown soup alleyways & firetrucks, not even one free beer ...

The same embittered rhetoric is very much part of Lordan's repertoire, so that poems like 'The Last Cathedral' or the prose-poem 'Surviving the Recession' or 'The Well', have the maniacal intensity of Ginsberg's original:

> A vast hollow full of extra gravities, the tug and voiding densities
> of a city worth of failure;
> the past, present and future of its absences and lack.

> Lack of eyes to watch, throats to cheers [*sic*], fists to shake,
> hands to come together ...
> — 'THE LAST CATHEDRAL'

Or:

> If you become homeless, join a library and order multiple copies of the onionist's cookbook. And the onanist's cockbook. But don't confuse the two. Don't cook your cock or slide a spring onion up your buttered arse, expecting a burst of colonial joy.

> Watch out for boredom, frustration, depression and tantrums. Keep smoking drinking and eating crisps and biscuits. Keep the television on ...
> — 'SURVIVING THE RECESSION'

Or:

Greed's our reason, cause and woe.
Our legacy is poisoning.

No water.
Nothing whatsoever left behind for me to drink.
                                    — 'THE WELL'

These are poems of clear and deliberate political and social critique which land more than a few blows on their targets. The violence and menace of *The Boy in the Ring* is even more strongly felt in *Invitation to a Sacrifice* where the title poem describes a rape, as does the child abuse in 'Nightmare Pastoral'. The bullying theme of 'The Boy in the Ring' continues in 'Bullies', while 'Somebody's got to do Somethin...' describes police violence. If these poems suggest something of the torn social fabric in Ireland today, then Lordan's descriptions of casual violence, use of multiple profanities and generally drug-riddled and alcohol-laden subject matter come as appropriate poetic fare in the current climate.

This having been said, in the latter half of the volume the rhetoric begins to weary the reader so that the scatological surrealism of the prose pieces in 'The Methods of the Enlightenment' has little impact. Indeed, one is tempted to agree with Grace Wells's analysis (writing in *The Stinging Fly*) that: 'Whereas *The Boy in the Ring* was a well-balanced read that tempered extremities, *Invitation to a Sacrifice* is decidedly off-kilter ... it is Bad-Bastard who takes the lead role, stamping heavy-fisted through the collection ...', in a way which, in places, obfuscates rather than convinces us of the seriousness of the book's political statement. Lordan might consider dampening his rhetoric for the next collection to ensure that the lyric balance of his first volume re-emerges.

Philip McDonagh is a poet of well-travelled erudition whose lyrical control and formal dexterity were amply shown in his first collection *Carraroe in Saxony* (Dedalus Press, 2003) and whose second collection *The Song the Oriole Sang* does not disappoint. These are meditative poems which take their starting point from foreign cultures, scenery, wildlife and customs which are interwoven with the poet's professional and personal life in a well-executed blend of the domestic and familial with the exotic. It is enough sometimes for McDonagh to evoke a place simply for the impression it made on him and, by turn, on us, his readers:

I shall remember Kerala
for how the disappearing moon
glanced in our faces, as if the sea

not far from Kottayam, in which
we watched for birds, was there by destiny.

– 'KERALA'

Or:

Laconic Lappish landscapes
of lakes, trees, rock –
how is it they display

a fantail subtlety, as if
a master's touch
found every shade in clay?

[...]

...We shall verify
in bog, brook, fell, flower
a handiwork that lives.

– 'IN LAPLAND'

Equally, McDonagh frequently includes personae in his poems to mediate the exotic or foreign locales he describes. It is as if, in the midst of a busy and business-driven world, men of affairs and diplomats should also pause to take stock of their environment. Thus, a feeling of imperial calm descends on the poem 'The Song the Oriole Sang' where an oriental governor Bai Juyi who 'was a mandarin / who governed provinces' nonetheless finds time to discuss 'the price of peonies' and to listen to 'the song the oriole sang'. Likewise, the medium-length poem 'Memories of an Ionian Diplomat' retains the same old-world atmosphere of old-fashioned diplomacy interwoven with historical and philosophical meditations on statecraft and the Macedonia question; but beyond this, the 'deep-mined privacy / of composition' strikes us so that the self-awareness of the diplomat and of the poet are aligned suggestively. It is no necessary contradiction to be a poet as well as a busy diplomat.

There is also a warmth and humanity here in poems which reach out towards the wider world. McDonagh remembers the British Secretary of State for Northern Ireland Mo Mowlam in the opening poem of the book 'Mo Díreach', whose deft handling of the early stages of the Peace Process he pays tribute to. In a sonnet sequence at the heart of the book 'Saving the Balloons', McDonagh celebrates the work of an orphanage in Delhi:

Our invitation is to all the children
of walking age, from 2 right up to 9,

for children's theatre, a banana-guzzling
elephant in the forecourt, Indian-style
tea: Limca, cakes, pakoras on green lawns.
    – 'SAVING THE BALLOONS'

Equally touching is 'Alumna' where the poet's daughter guides a green
turtle from the beach where it has hatched towards the surf and freedom
of the ocean, leading McDonagh to reflect on the lasting innocence of
certain natural cycles:

They say green turtles,
Living with luck a hundred years or more,
Come back in all their generations
To one shore;
As festivals
That fill our wells
Of commonality
And make new marriages,
Are bigger than ourselves ...
    – 'ALUMNA'

This sense of a world bigger than ourselves sets the tone for many of
McDonagh's personal, poetic and political meditations which are imbued
with a certain awe and humility. Despite this volume's peregrinations,
the poet concludes in Connemara echoing the Gaeilge of Máirtín Ó
Direáin in 'Water Is Best': 'candles could burn in every window / and
wanderers / find welcome, even now.' It is perhaps appropriate to conclude
such a well-travelled volume with a homecoming.

What McDonagh's verse lacks in directness and lyric concision, Ger
Reidy more than compensates for in poems which fizzle like fireworks
on a November evening. Reidy makes much out of his Mayo locales, but
not for geographic reasons of identity or belonging, but more as building
blocks for direct lyrical statements which often leave the reader astounded
at how much philosophic weight Reidy can give a short 15-20 line poem.
There are no meta-poetic tricks here. These are straightforward lyric
poems which yield their meanings without undue effort. To quote this or
that excerpt from Reidy is to do him a disservice. This volume deserves
to be read in its entirety with the same intense concentration which has
gone into the poems' making. Reidy avoids any pastoralism and his
Kavanagh-like realism and eye for the particular neither celebrates nor
condemns his own parish. As he writes in 'The Settlement': 'out here,
like everywhere / I have learned that this is all there is.' This reminds us
of Philip Larkin's famous line 'Here no elsewhere underwrites my

existence' (from 'The Importance of Elsewhere') and Reidy's poems echo the grounded concision of Larkin albeit without his customary gloom. Perhaps a happier comparison would be R S Thomas whose poems attain an astonishing lyrical amplitude out of the slightest of rural subject matters, as Reidy's do here.

While acknowledging the intrinsic differences of these three poets, each is successful, to a degree, on his own terms. These volumes may not reveal too many new tricks or new themes, but one is encouraged by the sincerity of each in putting his vision across in language which is vigorous, often original, and never dull.

Jonathan Ellis

LOVING LARKIN

Philip Larkin, *Letters to Monica*, edited by Anthony Thwaite (Faber and
Faber, 2010), hb £22.50.

Philip Larkin's life, or rather our idea of the life, is almost as well-known
as his poems. Since the publication of the *Selected Letters* in 1992 and
Andrew Motion's biography in 1993, several films and plays have examined
this life, nearly all focusing on his famously chaotic relationships with
women. There have been publications of his early poems, nearly all of his
critical writings, and most of his prose fiction, including several schoolgirl
stories written under the pseudonym of Brunette Coleman. Even a statue
has been created in his likeness. Likeability is not a quality one immediately
associates with Larkin. The publication of the *Selected Letters*, edited like
this volume by Anthony Thwaite, marks the moment at which not liking
Larkin became *de rigueur* for many academic critics. Tom Paulin's
assessment at the time, that the letters were 'a distressing and in many
ways revolting compilation which imperfectly reveals and conceals the
sewer under the national monument', is perhaps the most well-known
and certainly the most well-cited attack on Larkin the man as opposed to
Larkin the poet. In Lisa Jardine's opinion, Larkin's letters revealed both a
'casual, habitual racist and an easy misogynist'. 'We don't tend to teach
Larkin much in my department', she announced rather proudly.

Larkin scholars have perfected various lines of defence over the years
in answer to such criticisms. That individual letters are neither as racist
nor as misogynist as Paulin or Jardine believed. That he was basically
entertaining individual correspondents rather than revealing his 'true'
feelings. That letters are not to be trusted. Or, simply, that letters are not
as important as poems. As Martin Amis recently put it after having read
the volume of letters under review: 'Larkin's life was a failure; his work
was a triumph. That is all that matters. Because the work, unlike the life,
lives on.' Twenty years after the initial revelations about Larkin's life,
liking or not liking Larkin the person no longer seems at issue. We can
love 'the work' instead. Interestingly, Amis doesn't feel Larkin's *Letters to
Monica* is part of this body of work. 'His *Selected Letters* constitutes a literary event of the first order', he argues. 'The present book will remain a
literary curiosity.' For Amis, there is just too much Larkin and too little
Literature in *Letters to Monica*. The letters he values are those in which
prosaic life takes second place to poetic prose. He likes letters without
the life which is at least a little better than liking none of the letters at all.

I'd like to take issue here with both ways of reading Larkin's letters. For Paulin, Larkin's letters are not just reminders of Larkin's life. They reveal how that life was lived at its most basic level, 'the sewer' of the poet rather than his tower or turret. No room is admitted in Larkin's epistolary world for invention, mimicry or simply performance. Paulin's one-dimensional reading of Larkin's letters is all the more surprising given his interest in the art of letter writing as evidenced in a contemporaneous review of Elizabeth Bishop's *Selected Letters* in which he calls for 'a poetics of the familiar letter':

> Do letters possess what has been disdainfully termed "literarity"? Or do they, as I believe is true, construct themselves on an anti-aesthetic, a refusal of the literary? Is their rhetoric a rejection of rhetoric in the interests of brief, in-the-moment, authentic certainties? Are letters not written against posterity as throwaway, disposable, flimsy unique holographs which aim to flower once and once only in the recipient's reading and then disappear immediately? The merest suspicion that the writer is aiming beyond the addressee at posterity freezes a letter's immediacy and destroys its spirit. Posterity – the gathered jury of posthumous readers – feels cheated and refuses to be impressed.

Paulin's definition of good letter writing as an 'anti-aesthetic' form of literature that ignores 'posterity' is as applicable to Larkin as it is to Bishop. Both poets arguably loved letter writing precisely because it was a form of writing not immediately linked to publication, even as both knew that posthumous publication of their correspondence was probably inevitable. The 'spoken texture' he admires in Bishop's correspondence is just as present in Larkin's. Letters that exist in their own right, not as 'a staging post towards the poem' but 'as a type of Imagist poem', are as common in his *Selected Letters* as hers. Whereas in Bishop's case Paulin celebrates the autonomy and uniqueness of every letter as yet another art form in which Bishop excels – he describes 'each letter' as a 'historic moment' – in Larkin's case the letters are read as a whole rather than individually and are then used to belittle both poems and poet. His employment of Larkin's letters as a glossary on the poems, as a prose version of them, is, in other words, completely contrary to both the method and spirit of reading letters he advocates elsewhere.

Amis's defence of Larkin has its blind spots too. His reasons for privileging the *Selected Letters* over *Letters to Monica*, for example, appear to me completely unfounded. According to Amis, 'The fact that Larkin made little effort with Monica is everywhere apparent in these pages [...]. Here, Larkin's prose is habitually perfunctory and pressureless'. The sheer volume of correspondence from which Thwaite has prepared this book (nearly two thousand letters, telegrams and postcards) suggests Larkin did at least make *some* effort with Monica. As Alan Jenkins points out, 'that works out at an average of one a week', not including letters lost or mislaid by Monica in the years after Larkin's death. While Larkin's prose is perhaps more 'perfunctory' here than in the *Selected Letters*, particularly when he was keeping Monica at arm's length during his relationship with Maeve Brennan, Amis's characterisation of the whole book in such terms is unfair. After all, first images from some of Larkin's finest poems, 'The Whitsun Weddings', 'An Arundel Tomb' and 'Cut Grass' among them, begin life in letters to Monica. She had first sight of many other poems too. In addition to this, Monica received some of Larkin's best unpublished prose on a range of subjects. Some of this material is to be expected of Larkin. His obsession with death, for example: 'One of the quainter quirks of life is that we shall never know who dies on the same day as we do ourselves.' Or his opinions on work: 'How little our careers express what lies in us, and yet how much time they take up.' Much else is genuinely moving and surprising. Who could have guessed about an early 'prejudice for the left' rather than the right? Who knew he was such a Katherine Mansfield fan? That one of his favourite books, given to him by Monica, was Frances Hodgson Burnett's *The Secret Garden*? That one of the things he liked most about the book was its message about life? According to Larkin, *The Secret Garden* 'calls on everyone to put aside distrusts and shrinking-back, and live to the utmost while life is for the having'. Why does Amis overlook this and other writing in the book? The answer, as Amis himself admits, appears to be a very personal dislike of Monica – 'a robust and comparatively wordly blonde, with well-shaped bones (but ogreish teeth)' – that prevents him from seeing any good in Larkin's relationship with her, even when that relationship was conducted mainly in letters, an art form in which Amis acknowledges Larkin to be a master. In failing to see what Larkin sees in Monica ('the most frightening' of all of Larkin's women according to Amis), he refuses to see what anyone can see in any letter written to her.

Just as liking (or not liking) Larkin the person should not lead to a dismissal of Larkin the letter writer or Larkin the poet, so liking (or not liking) Monica should be beside the point when assessing Larkin's correspondence to her. Unlike Amis, I never met Monica Jones, though I was living in Hull when she was still alive (she died, an alcoholic by all accounts, in 2001). My knowledge of her character is, like most people's, almost entirely mediated via Larkin (Kingsley Amis readers might also have 'met' a version of her in the character of Margaret Peel in *Lucky Jim*). Larkin met Monica at University College, Leicester, in autumn 1946, when they were both twenty-four; he was the newly appointed Assistant Librarian and she was a recently appointed Assistant Lecturer. Both had been at Oxford, though they had never met there (in 'Poem about Oxford' Larkin describes a 'city we shared without knowing'). Both had First Class degrees in English. Both had been born in the same year, 1922, and came from relatively similar middle-class backgrounds. Monica was an only child. Larkin had an older sister, but due to differences in age and character, felt an only child too. In terms of their personalities, both preferred their own company to that of other people. Both enjoyed listening to the radio (the *Archers* is frequently discussed). Both liked Beatrix Potter. Neither enjoyed work. Neither felt entirely comfortable about their own bodies nor about sex. Both drank to relax, sometimes to excess. Although they spent nearly all of their holidays together and odd weekends, Larkin never proposed marriage though it is one of the main topics of discussion between them, even before the break-up of his on-off engagement to another woman (Ruth Bowman) in 1950. In a letter written on 22 January 1955, for example, Monica asked if Larkin '*were* marrying [...] would you rather marry me than anybody else?' Larkin did not exactly reassure her. While admitting that 'I would sooner marry you than *anyone* else I know', he also wondered 'whether I do more than just like you very, very much and find it flattering and easy to stay with you instead of, well, behaving as folks do, rushing after other people who take their fancy – of course, very few people *do* take my fancy; the ones that do are "quite impossible"'. 'I think what frightens me most about marriage', he continued in a letter sent a month later, 'is the passing-a-law-never-to-be-alone-again side of it'. The conversation didn't end there. On 6 August 1955 Larkin is still toying with the idea of marriage, though in equally unpromising terms:

> Do you think if we married we should be the same, & live in a semi-detached house called "Oakdene" & advance "sound parish views"? That wd be awful, wouldn't it? There would be a piano next door, played by someone who changed the treble but not the bass. The bakelite handle of the "french window" ... The kitchen audible in the lavatory & vice versa ... but this is a horror story. I'm sure we'd do better than that.

Joking aside, one wonders how Monica must have felt reading letter after letter in this vein. Indeed, for all the time shared on holiday and through letter writing, they didn't live permanently together until 1983 when Larkin finally invited her to live in his house in Hull, where he looked after her until his own death in December 1985. 'They had', according to Thwaite, 'settled into something close to marriage'. Close but not quite.

Given their compatibility – Thwaite believes they 'fed each other's misery' – why didn't Larkin and Monica ever marry? Larkin provides several answers to this question in his correspondence with Monica, as we have already seen. His poetry also addresses this dilemma in various fictional forms and voices, most memorably in 'Self's the Man', 'Dockery and Son' and 'Vers de Société'. But what did Monica make of his lifelong hesitancy? Why, when she learned of his relationships with other women, sometimes through poems addressed to them, didn't she break finally with him? There is no clear answer to any of these questions. Monica's voice, like most female addressees of famous, frequently male correspondents, is more or less silenced in this book. Thwaite includes some sentences from Monica's letters in footnotes to Larkin's own prose, but nothing more. The collection acquired by the Bodleian Library in 2004 from the Monica Jones Estate is, it is worth stating, not just a collection of Philip Larkin's letters. It also contains Monica's own correspondence to Larkin. In an ideal world, or at least in a world where arts funding could provide grants for such an editing project, we might be reading *Letters To and From Monica* rather than just Larkin's side of the correspondence. From the evidence of this book, Monica's letters clearly prompted and provoked not just Larkin's epistolary gifts but his poetic ones too. She is the unnamed addressee in many of Larkin's most iconic poems: the 'friend' in 'I Remember, I Remember', the implied lover in 'Talking in Bed', and, in the closing line of 'An Arundel Tomb', the subject of Larkin's most emotional tribute ('What will survive of us is love'). Other poems appear to be at least partially written in Monica's voice. It is striking, for example, to read an extract from Monica's letter on 18 August 1955 in which she comments on the poem 'Mr Bleaney' as sounding not just 'like you – yr catalogue of the room's shortcomings', but also 'like you & like me'. Perhaps poems formerly considered quintessentially Larkinesque owe something to Monica too?

The book blurb announces rather disingenuously that a 'selection from Larkin's side of the correspondence [...] tells both sides of their story'. I doubt Monica would agree. In the early 1960s, when Larkin was in the midst of his affair with Maeve Brennan, she regularly scribbled notes in the margin of his letters disputing his version of events. In one letter urging her not to 'be miserable over this Maeve business', Monica was particularly furious. 'Note the style, the irony of style, & no intention of doing anything like what is said', she wrote in the margin. Who are notes like this written for? Presumably not Larkin who knew exactly how she felt given the apologetic note to nearly all of his correspondence to Monica at this time. Perhaps a posthumous reader? In 31 July 1964 Larkin again encourages her not to 'apologise for crying – cry all you need'. Then, one sentence after admitting to feeling 'guilty about Maeve', he talks of wishing 'I were with you now, expecially if you are wearing your mauve dress'. It is difficult to see how Monica would have missed this 'Maeve/mauve' slip. What did she say in reply? The answer lies not in this book but in the Bodleian Library.

In his introduction to the book, Thwaite suggests that Monica's career at Leicester was 'marked in particular by two things':

> First, there was the panache of her lecturing, in which, for example, she would wear a Scottish tartan when talking about *Macbeth*. (Some were rather shocked by her. A former student, now in her late seventies, recalled: "In my then opinion, Miss Jones was very suspiciously blonde, very highly made-up, and talked a great deal without asking our opinion of anything. All that was excusable, but what really upset me was that her tops were much too low at the front"). Second, Monica regarded publishing as a bit showy, and she never in fact published anything during the whole of her academic career.

In today's academic climate, Monica's failure to publish anything over a thirty-year career would probably be a sackable, or at least a pensionable offence. Yet perhaps Monica's letters, even in an extremely abridged form, *are* her publications. Certainly, there are very few academics who can lay claim to having seen the first drafts of so many iconic poems or whose opinions were trusted enough to contemplate revising lines even after they had been published (Larkin changed the word 'litany' to 'liturgy' in 'Water' following Monica's advice). Whether or not she was Larkin's 'muse' – Alan Jenkins considers she was 'that much more valuable thing, a sensitive and trusted sounding board' – she was at least his most constant and certainly his sharpest critic, both of his personality and his poems.

Putting Monica to one side for a moment, as Larkin himself frequently did, what else are these letters about? As one might expect from even a cursory reading of his poems, one of their main preoccupations is Larkin's fear of death, a preoccupation deepened both by his father's sudden death in 1948 and his mother's increasing dependence on him as the years passed. 'I seem to walk on a transparent surface', he wrote to Monica on 12 March 1957, 'and see beneath me all the bones and wrecks and tentacles that will eventually claim me: in other words, old age, incapacity, loneliness, death of others & myself'. Astonishingly, Larkin was just thirty-four years old when he wrote this. In a further fascinating letter dated 13 November 1956, Larkin attempted to make sense of his parents' apparently loveless marriage, one of the main sources of his own despair about life, by likening their relationship to that between Thomas Hardy and his first wife, Emma Gifford:

> (The figure of my father, the shy, not over-robust, Edwardian clerk pressing T.H. [Thomas Hardy] on all his friends, is unlike the man I knew. I think he was a terrific romantic; & my mother was the

equivalent of Emma Lavinia Gifford. Poor father! My heart bleeds for him. What a terrible fate!) I think there's something quite frightening about all the widows, living effortlessly on, with their NH specs & teeth & wigs, cackling chara-loads of them, while in the dingy cemeteries their shadowy men lie utterly effaced – I want to write a poem on this called *To my mother & the memory of my father*, but can't / daren't.

Hardy famously mourned his first wife's death in the collection, *Poems of 1912-13*, though he was only able to write of Emma in this way once she had actually died. There is a sense in which Larkin's own ambivalent feelings for his mother are similar to those experienced by Hardy for Emma. The difference for Larkin of course is that his 'Emma' almost outlived him, and certainly her death coincided with an almost immediate failure of poetic nerve (Eva died on 17 November 1977, Larkin finished his last great poem, 'Aubade', on 29 November 1977). For all his complaints, in other words, his imagination somehow needed his mother's continuing presence. This ambivalence can obviously be seen even in the draft title of the poem Larkin couldn't or 'daren't' write. '*To my mother & the memory of my father*' makes the speaker sound an elegist of both parents, even when only one parent was actually dead. The mother comes first in the poet's list, but not his memory of her. It is as if she exists, as she perhaps did for Larkin, in an eternal present, one of those widows, 'living effortlessly on'.

Larkin's mother is the answer to many questions about the poet's attitude to love and marriage. Indeed, nearly all of his denunciations of marriage to Monica follow his annual summer 'holiday' with Eva. On 1 September 1951, for instance, he wrote of married life in terms of 'the constant lack of solitude, the never-being able-to-relax, not at midnight, or 3 a.m. or any time of day'. On Christmas night 1953, another extended stay with Eva provoked the following comment: 'Home, I think, might be defined as the place where one is bored and irritated – and, of course, embarrassed, too, sometimes – or perhaps the place where reality is strongest, which is very much the same thing'. In December 1954 Larkin continues to mull over his feelings about 'the present situation':

Admitted, my mother is nervy, cowardly, obsessional, boring, grumbling, irritating, self pitying. It's no use telling her to alter: you might as well tell a sieve to hold water. On the other hand, she's kind, timid, unselfish, loving, and upset both by losing her husband rather early & by being seventy (next month) with both her children showing *marked* reluctance to live with her. [...] Am I, ultimately, on her side? God knows! In my heart of hearts, I'm on no one's side but my own.

Monica, to her eternal credit, warned Larkin not to give in to Eva's desire to live with her son on his return to England (he was due to take up the post of Librarian at Hull in March 1955). 'Don't be robbed of your soul', she urged him in a long letter. 'I don't mean by that exactly, simply, don't live with your Mother; if you could do it without being robbed, that would not count, but can you, can you even live at all without it; can you?' Larkin attempts to answer this question again and again in the letters to Monica, and in several poems too. Yet in his heart of hearts, as he himself admits in the Christmas letter (not a particularly seasonal greeting for Monica), he was on no one's side but his own.

For all Larkin's talk of death and loneliness, these are not ultimately lifeless letters. On the contrary, thinking of death often appears to bring out the best in Larkin, the best in terms of his facility for creating memorable language rather than any false cheeriness about everyday existence. In a letter from 15 July 1971, for example, Larkin reflects poignantly on some of the reasons for his depression:

> ...the prospect of life, or what's left of it, stretches before me (to use my favourite quotation) like an infinitely tiring staircase. One learns nothing and forgets nothing, like the Bourbons. It's ghastly. I wish I could forget things. Or, if I've got to remember them, I wish I could remember pleasant things as well as unpleasant things. I suppose pleasant things make no impression.

The letter is arguably a companion piece to the poem, 'Cut Grass', completed six weeks earlier on 3 June 1971, with its more or less identical reflection on life as a brief moment of delight before month after month of long, slow dying. In most cases in Larkin's work, the letter comes before the poem that seems connected to it. In the case of 'Whitsun Weddings', for example, Larkin's August 1955 note on returning home by train and 'at every station, Goole, Doncaster, Retford, Newark, [seeing] importunate wedding parties, gawky & vociferous', predates the finished poem by more than three years (the poem was finished on 18 October 1958). The boundaries between letters and poems are often paper-thin, as various epistolary critics have shown. For authors like Larkin, any form of text might at some stage become literature, whether it began life as an advert ('Sunny Prestatyn'), inscription ('MCMXIV') or letter ('Maiden Name'). Equally, poems, while finished, can often be added to in letters, as here. In this sense, one might see them not just as messages to Monica, but as postscripts for readers too. In a further letter on 'Cut Grass', for example, Larkin admitted to feeling anxious about the poem's change in tone 'about line 6': 'I hear a kind of wonderful Elgar river-music take over, for wch the words are just an excuse. [...]. Do you see what I mean?

There's a point at wch the logical sense of the poem ceases to be added to, and it continues only as a succession of images. I like it all right, but for once I'm not a good judge.' Such letters ask first for Monica's reassurance. He wants her to 'judge' the poem favourably by return of post. At the same time, letters so carefully composed on the subject of poetry are almost certainly written to future readers too, both as a clue to Larkin's mood as well as a message on how to read this particular poem, for 'music' rather than 'sense'.

As much as these are letters about and for posterity, they are also written in and to the moment. In this sense, they belong to both the aesthetic and anti-aesthetic traditions of letter writing outlined by Paulin above. Their momentariness is particularly to the fore when talking about food or drink. Monica appears to have spent much of the Fifties and Sixties advising Larkin on how to make ration-bought meat edible. Much drinking goes on off-stage as well. The letters also reprint several of Larkin's drawings, many of which depict his various lodgings over the years. A list of Larkin's holiday destinations – Bournemouth, King's Lynn, Pocklington, Sark, York – makes clear how foreign even the idea of foreign travel was in postwar Britain, even for somebody relatively well-off. In such details, one gets a vivid sense of what it must have been like to live and work in Fifties Britain. More than this, one also gets a sense of what it must have been like to be Larkin. There is a famous letter from John Keats to his brother and sister-in-law in America when he describes the very moment of writing the letter – 'the candles are burnt down and I am using the wax taper – which has a long snuff on it – the fire is at its last click – I am sitting with my back to it with one foot rather askew upon the rug and the other with the heel a little elevated from the carpet' – as an attempt to make present his own life for them. 'Could I see the same thing done of any great Man long since dead it would be a great delight: as to know in what position Shakespeare sat when he began "To be or not to be" – such thing[s] become interesting from distance of time or place.' Larkin's letters are full of such moments too as, for example, when a brown mouse surprises him: 'While writing all that', he tells Monica on 12 November 1951, 'I noticed a *brown mouse* creep out behind the fireplace & edge along the wainscoting – not very nice! First time I've seen him. He *scuttled* back on realising he wasn't alone. This depresses me rather – Beatrix Potter's all very well in print but...'

In later years, as Larkin became more famous and as the prospect of his letters being published grew more real, such Keatsian moments are rarer. He makes jokes about enjoying 'a Larkin afternoon' in the countryside or his latest 'discovery in Larkin studies'. Yet even when Larkin is being ironic about his letter-writing skills, he still manages to be both memorable and poignant as here:

I don't seem to be able to write you the interesting sort of letter I should like to – if I lived in the golden age of English letter writing, and had nothing to do but snuff the candles, draw the curtains, and lodge the kettle on the fire, I'm sure I could do much better. "Past Turvey's Mill on my walk, dyd see a *Hare*," etc. A pity we can't live in our imaginations! My kitchen wireless has gone wrong, so I eat my meals in silence – having heard the Archers in the sitting room. All being well, I shall see you next weekend. I don't know whether I shall appear by six – I'll let you know.

As Keats looks back to Shakespeare in his letter on 12 March 1819, so Larkin in this letter, written on 23 November 1967, seems to evoke the very image of Keats in the midst of writing his letter with 'nothing to do but snuff the candles'. Larkin frequently apologised about his letter writing to Monica. 'I'm sorry if I neglect to answer things in your letters', he wrote on 8 December 1956, 'to some extent I've "always" done it: my parents, & Kingsley [Amis], complained similarly. There may be several reasons – carelessness, forgetfulness perhaps, tho' I *always* write with your *last* letter beside me'. In a much later letter, from 26 October 1972, he is still apologising. 'This letter is really weak with fatigue. I would have telephoned, but a letter is more lasting, & I hope to have one from you. You are a brilliant letter writer.' One can't help but feel Larkin is protesting a little too much here. Even (or perhaps especially) in the letter that proposes not to be 'interesting', one cannot fail to experience all the emotions that great literature depends on, amusement and sadness chief among them. As in the poem, 'I Remember, I Remember', when Larkin evokes a golden childhood that he can't remember, so here, he evokes 'a golden age of letter writing' that no longer exists. Yet, in his imagination just as much as in ours, the golden age of letter writing lives again every time we read a letter by Keats, or I would argue, by Larkin. The image of Larkin, the kitchen wireless 'gone wrong', eating his meals in silence, is an arresting one, and just as memorable in its own way as the image of Keats with his back to the fire and his foot 'askew upon the rug'.

Will Larkin's correspondence ever be seen as the equal of his poems? Is he a writer whose letters will eventually enhance or harm his reputation? Will we ever love his letters like those of Keats or will they be allowed to go periodically out of print like those by Joyce? It is too early to say. For the moment, one can and should champion Anthony Thwaite's meticulous editing of this book, part of his lifelong championing of Larkin's poetry. Although he has a minor role in these letters, he has had a major role in Larkin's posthumous life. In addition to editing two volumes of Larkin's letters, he has also edited two editions of the poetry as well. It must not have been easy to reduce the 7,500 pages sold to the Bodleian to a shade under 500 pages here. As Adam Mars-Jones points out, that 'represents a heroic effort of whittling'. As important as this, he has managed to present the letters in a way that does justice to the various sides of Larkin's character, those we might admire and those we might dislike. Although one might describe *Letters to Monica* as an epistolary novel with one of the main protagonists more or less edited out, Thwaite gives just about enough glances of Monica's personality to at least imagine what her life might look like.

The book's title, *Letters to Monica*, echoes another famous collection of letters to one woman, Franz Kafka's *Letters to Milena*. Both Milena and Monica arguably inspired Kafka's and Larkin's best letters, and perhaps the best side of their characters. Larkin compared his more famous friendship with Kingsley Amis to that between two fourth formers ('I've always needed this "fourth form friend", with whom I can pretend that things are *not* as I know they are'). He used to sign letters to Amis using variations on the phrase 'Yours bum', as in 'Lower paid bum' or 'A series of six programmes by Seamus bum'. Larkin and Monica's own monikers for each other were a lot more whimsical. Larkin referred to Monica as a rabbit, she referred to him as a seal. What analogy best fits their relationship? Larkin and Monica were more than friends and often lovers, but they were permanently together for just a couple of years, and that at the very end of Larkin's life. If one were sentimental, one might evoke the stone figures in 'An Arundel Tomb', the earl still 'holding her hand'. A more truthful image is probably that offered in 'Talking in Bed' of a couple attempting to find words 'at once true and kind, / Or not untrue and not unkind'. Larkin and Monica, like the poem's final line, were two double negatives lying side by side. In the final analysis of their letters, one cannot tell who is telling the truth anymore, which of them was more kind, or less unkind, than the other. What will survive of them is not exactly love, as Larkin puts it in 'An Arundel Tomb', but letters, some of which are loving, some of which are not. One can't / daren't not read them.

Eamon Grennan

NEWS OF THE WORLD

Derek Mahon, *An Autumn Wind* (Gallery Press, 2010), €11.95.

Being asked to review Derek Mahon's latest volume for *PIR* prompted a
stroll among the earlier books, all the way back to *Night Crossing* of 1968
(*annus mirabilis* for other reasons as well). This in turn produced a feeling –
which I always have on re-reading him – of exhilaration at the richness of
his art and craft, the sense of being from the very start in the hands of a
master, one who learned his trade more quickly than most. (Even
Longley, speedy enough himself, has to recall how in TCD he couldn't
'settle comfortably' into the profession of college poet, 'Once Derek
arrived reciting Rimbaud, giving names / To the constellations over the
Examination Hall', and asking for the loan of a typewriter). Dark matter
with a singing style has always been his mode. As he said about Malcolm
Lowry (*Under the Volcano* was an important early love of his), 'The message
is despair but the style sings of hope', a tense yet seemingly effortless
musicality he also found in the plangent prose sentences of Scott Fitzgerald.

In addition there's always, no matter the subject, Mahon's irony shim-
mering over everything he does. Mordant or playful, it can be sporadic,
but it's always a constituent of the Mahon *ton*, a cocktail – stirred *and*
shaken – part Ecclesiastes, part Swift, part Shakespearean romance. He
has always, too, seemed so much a grown-up – if always with a twinkle
of mischief in his artist's eye, irony never far from the sober truths he
keeps bringing to our attention. He's persistently imagining 'the ideal
society', but with a properly sceptical sense of its impossibility for humans
as we are. It is something in a distant future: a return to some pure state
of human goodwill in a restored, refreshed natural world, with the gods
(whoever or whatever they might be) as benevolent overseers. 'I trace the
future', he says in 'The Sea in Winter' (1978), 'in a colour-scheme, /
Colours we scarcely dare to dream':

> One day, the day each one conceives –
> The day the Dying Gaul revives,
> The day the girl among the trees
> Strides through our wrecked technologies,
> The stones speak out, the rainbow ends,
> The wine goes round among the friends,
> The lost are found, the parted lovers
> Lie at peace beneath the covers.

Many of Mahon's enduring virtuoso touches can be observed here: lithe control of the tetrameter through end-stop and enjambment; moulding of line and sentence into the satisfying stanza shape; decisive but not mechanical iambic movement; mix of casual statement with a largesse of image; rhythmic poise and relaxed rhymes; the traffic between mono- and polysyllabic words; the unexpected conjunction of mythic and scientific; a vision that takes art and everyday reality into a single, steady embrace.

Another sustained trait in Mahon is his discretion *vis-à-vis* biographical intimacy, 'confessional' revelation. In his work, momentary data of the biographical self are mostly turned into emblems of a life lived with supreme self-awareness. Even the crisis points – drink, disintegration – are maintained at arm's length by discretion of style, never descending into the merely confessional. For Mahon, the tense moments of scarifying self-revelation and self knowledge prompt lyric lucidity rather than auto-biographical excursions. In the early work, indeed, the persona-speaker-subject of many poems is not necessarily the biographical self, but some metamorphic 'I' who is a creature all imagination – now the 'last of the Fire Kings',' now a witness to universal decay, now an artist like Edvard Munch or Van Gogh, now a generalised inhabitant – witty and aware – of Northern Ireland, now a representative 'poet', now a citizen of the world, a cultural onlooker, part anchorite, part flâneur. As the culture canvas in later work becomes more crowded, however, he can shift from being a quiet witness to a garrulous, insomniac commentator upon the sprawling, mixed-up, multi-levelled nature of a world gone global (in *The Yellow Book*, for example).

Mahon's many masks, though, have allowed him to compose a coherent account of this world as he knows it, and his own – sometimes solitary, sometimes accompanied (by family, by lover, by friend) – restless, vigilant, responsive place in it. It is, so, the world we all know and live in (of emotions, politics, culture, and all the non-human 'mute phenomena'), seen from the perspective of an exacting, scrupulous, human gaze that manages to be at the same time both undeceived and hopeful. And what-ever their subject, the poems always pulsate with a refined sense of a voice – quiet, careful, watchful, intense – that embodies a position regarding the world, a position deliberately and at the same time circum-stantially and existentially taken by an articulate, civilised, mannerly but not mannered, speaker.

Spoken language, indeed, is at the heart of Mahon's take on the world, heard in his ability to shift quickly gears and levels – from brash colloquial (Irish, English, American) to 'cultured', to refined, to mandarin. He is, in other words, a master of his own well-tempered speech music, capable of embracing intimate biographical details on the one hand and cosmic human truths on the other – thoughts (he has thoughts, not ideas) about time and space ('the existential stark / Face of the cosmic dark'), about politics, the fate of the world, the state of nature. Yeats could manage this too, but Mahon avoids sounding 'Yeatsian' by going back to the habits of Jonson, Marvell and Donne (as well as Swift), back to their ways of folding sentence, line, and stanza into syntactically muscular musical units. On the more modern side, he's tuned by MacNeice who can turn a mean pentameter (as in 'Eclogue for Christmas') and by Lowell's handling of the tetrameter line, the powerful couplet-based stanzas of 'Waking Early Sunday Morning'. Mahon's is a speech both refined and colloquial, a speech manner equally at home with cultural patois and something more philosophically inflected. Such a confluence of forces gives his verse buoyancy and speed, so that whatever the subject matter, however deep and dark the content, his expression possesses an almost debonair light-footedness all its own. (Of course Heaney, Longley, Ní Chuilleanáin, Muldoon and others all have their own ways of blending speech with their own kind of rhythmic lyricism, their own kind of music, but only Mahon's carries us along at so speedy a clip. An interesting essay might tackle their differences in this respect – examining sources, influences, and consequences). Maybe only the matter in a poem like 'Dawn at St Patrick's' eludes, in its irregular seven-lined stanzas, such buoyancy – grave-tuned as it is by its material, its sobered self-knowing.

Aside from its vehicle of speech, then, there is in the realm of 'spirit' values a constant bright thread running through Mahon's work, an articulate conviction – while not as bald as Éluard's that there is 'another world present in this one', nor as religiously inflected or quietist as Kavanagh's 'To look on is enough/ In the business of love' – that there nonetheless exists imaginatively a zone where the actual in all its gritty immediacies can shimmer with a certain immanent possibility. It is a zone of possibility distinguished by what he calls (in 'Courtyards in Delft') an 'oblique light on the trite', in which no transcendent reality offers itself to us, but in which we have the chance at moments of seeing into the real, and seeing it is good, even if that good lies in some undetermined future, or even in some non-human world of tree, leaf, water or other innocent material forces and facts, man-made as well as natural. Such an understanding of the world, I guess, is what draws him to poets like Bonnefoy and Jaccottet (the 'gravity and grace' of whose critical style he has admired), and to such a formulation as Jaccottet's *'ce monde n'est que la crête / d'un invisible incendie.'* On the other hand, no one has performed more convincingly as the melancholy, witty philosopher of history, the amused dystopian with his view of our predicament from 'out in the void':

> Welcome to the planet,
> its fluorescent beers

buzzing in the desolate

silence of the spheres.

    – 'THE TERMINAL BAR'

But while his wishing for the radiance of 'the first week of creation', his desiring a world renewed by restoring nature to its innocent pre-lapsarian condition, may be seen as (in his own word) 'naive,' yet it is just such a palpable, emotionally persuasive aspiration that is also one of the most human, humane energies in the poetry.

Although Mahon's grave and witty, mordant and amused, elegiac and critical imagination is a whispering gallery alive – both in sentiment and in verse technique – with Marvell's 'But always at my back I hear / Time's wingèd chariot hurrying near', Lowell's 'Pity the planet, all joy gone / from this sweet volcanic cone,' and Stevens' 'The maker's rage to order words of the sea'; and although in addition he would no doubt acknowledge such ghostly presences as the lyrical and quotidian MacNeice, as well as Beckett, Auden, and, in the shadowy background, Yeats – still, in terms of the texture of the verse itself, no line of Mahon's could now be mistaken for that of any other poet. There is such a bracing poise to each line, and then a lovely velocity as the lines follow one another down the page, each one accumulating another unit of thought utterly absorbed and articulated by a unit of rhythm. I read back into his early work, and so many lines are like little flares in the mind, reminding me of their first impact, the sense of 'he's done it' (usually accompanied by the unavoidable teeth-gritting admiration – common enough among his contemporaries, some of whom knew his lines by heart – of 'how does he do it?'). And in this new volume, *An Autumn Wind* that blows forty years and more from *Night Crossing,* it is pure satisfaction (beyond teeth-gritting now, a bit late for that), to be engaged yet again by poems that ignite, that detonate with something of that same earliest excitement.

It happens when I come across singing lines that bring, like few others can bring, thought and music together with a kind of classical finesse one might associate with the likes of Marvell's lyric sweetness and tough grace, along with the speedy insouciance and colloquial dash – indignant, though not savagely so – of Swift.

What for me is impressive about this latest collection, so, what I love about it, is how many of the earlier (and constant) notes I've mentioned are here struck – in refreshed combinations, but all with the same distinct, satisfying pitch and timbre. As much singer, satirist, utopian/dystopian as ever, Mahon manages to conduct in these poems a small lyric orchestra (rhythms poised, diction deft and surprising, panoptic eye ever-keen), while at the same time striking at the heart of cultural breakdown. As peripatetic in this work as in earlier volumes, he moves from place to place (Kinsale, Ithaca, Nerja, Delhi, Lanzarote, New York, the Skelligs, back to Kinsale) at times casting a cold eye (warmed by a characteristic lyric grace) on exemplary spectacles of contemporary decay, stupidity, and greed, (inheriting part of his social passion from MacNeice, but with a greater lyric flair and a wider data canvas, and a more deeply, more philo-sophically ramifying, response), at other times simply savouring the local – fauna, flora, human traces – and shaping even 'the most unpromising / material ... into a living thing.'

One of the three parts of this collection, too ('River of Stars'), is composed of translations from Chinese poets. In addition, the volume contains poems 'after' (Mahon's way of allowing for some freedom in his translations) Rimbaud, Quevedo, Baudelaire, Tomás Rua Ó Súilleabháin, and 'the fictitious Hindi poet Gopal Singh', for whom Mahon supplies a brief biography. Like his poems of cultural voyaging (in which he serves, it seems, as a magnet for all kinds of cultural phenomena and bric-a-brac), translations have always provided Mahon with a way out of the self into the world (where, like Stephen Dedalus's Shakespeare he will, of course, meet himself). The translations, so, are an intrinsic part of his *oeuvre*. In their manners, as well as in their various subject matters (for which, I suspect, they have been chosen), they allow him to continue, extend and deepen his own restlessly sustained encounter with the world. Like Yeatsian masks, they allow him to be himself:

> An autumn wind shivers my walking stick
> but peace of mind resides in ferns, flowers,
>
> music and daily habit for equilibrium,
> regular exercise to keep up the strength.
> — 'AUTUMN FIELDS'

The 'River of Stars' section (although not a series of haiku) reminds also of Mahon's fascination with the manners of haiku (remember 'The Snow Party' and other three-line stanza poems in the earlier work, like 'An Image Out of Beckett'), with haiku's rapt attention to the actual, its reverence for the concrete detail, its wish to make no judgmental gestures. Thus, it's a kind of counterpoint to the 'documentary' poems like 'The Hudson Letter' and 'The Yellow Book', in which his judgment impulses are up front. It might be said indeed that he as a poet pendulums between the pole of judgment and that of pure accommodating observa-tion.

What so many of the poems in *An Autumn Wind* show, too, is that while he is a scrupulous observer of simple facts, Mahon is also endlessly alert to the kind of allusive possibility that transforms fact into a textured demonstration of consciousness itself, into 'the very shape of thought' at work. In doing such work, he achieves a spry gravitas all his own.

Experiencing, thinking about, reading his way into a thunder shower, for example, he sees that 'All human life is there' (the phrase may allude to an ad for the English newspaper, *News of the World*). Whether with something as simple (perhaps) as weather, or something as large and complex as the jigsaw condition of American culture or the state of the nation of which he is a citizen, Mahon is always a close reader, one who offers his own idiosyncratically angled 'news of the world'.

Given the season of its title, the volume has many reminders of mortality and age (Mahon himself will be seventy this year). There's a tribute to 'Synge Dying,' in addition to well-crafted birthday poems for Montague, Longley, and Heaney, and an affectionate elegy for Jimmy Simmons – a sort of late example of a form in which Mahon has, going all the way back to 'Beyond Howth Head,' excelled, the letter poem – with in this case its memorial praise for the dead poet:

> The gulls still scream there on the roof
> as if they miss your voice, as if
> disconsolate for the cheery sight
> of their blithe poet stepping out
> in his trademark tweed overcoat –
> a nonchalant rebel, *blasé*, bluff,
> constantly singing, born to dance.
>   – 'ART AND REALITY'

In ways *An Autumn Wind* composes Mahon's own mutability cantos ('perpetual change and flux / are the true element'), at once celebrating and seeing the limitations of the world. And if at times the idealist's conclusions and injunctions and 'pious hopes' may be a touch too easy (see the ends of 'Blueprint' and 'A Quiet Spot,' for example), still the underlying, inspiriting vision itself to which they belong – with its profound sense of the law of universal change – achieves here again, as it always has, conviction. Given this, I can only imagine that the speech of Edmund Spenser's 'Nature,' in the Mutabilitie Cantos that conclude *The Faerie Queene*, is close to Mahon's imagination – its sixteenth-century mixture of realism and religious hope finding secular echoes in his own binocular Twenty-first century vision:

> 'I well consider all that ye have sayd,
> And find that all things stedfastness doe hate
> And changed be: yet being rightly wayd,
> They are not changed from their first estate;
> But by their change their being doe dilate:
> And turning to themselves at length againe,
> Doe worke their own perfection so by fate:

> Then over them Change doth not rule and raigne;
> But they raigne over Change, and doe their states maintaine.'

'What do we worship, now the gods are gone?' Mahon asks at one point. It's a question that has preoccupied him from the start, positing as it does a post-belief universe of the purely secular, and the possibility in it for the presence of something that 'used be called soul' (as a character says in Lowry's *Under the Volcano*). His work offers, without dogma or definition, not so much an answer, as a series of considered meditations of varying lyric intensity upon the question. In the fine poem, 'A Building Site' – in its mix of the gritty actual and the good dream – Mahon persists in his allegiance to something that goes back at least to that 'oblique light on the trite' illuminating 'Courtyards in Delft'. It is, he says, scrutinising things with his usual mix of compassion and panache:

> A grim summer, but if
> fortuitous light strikes
> the rubble and a sun-spoke
> pierces a cloud rift
> the meaning becomes clear.

And the meaning, as it turns out, is:

> a momentary, oblique
> vision of an unknown
> eternal dispensation,
> the infinite republic
> of primary creation.

One could spend a fair while doing some close reading of these short, packed lines. I won't. It's enough to see in their economy not only the persistence of Mahon's way into the world, but also the distance he has travelled (while holding to his course) in compact, articulate understanding of that world. One can simply salute him in his own words for 'a real thing well done / with real significance' ('New Space') – for something that sustains, as his best work always has, 'the venerable ideal / of spirit lodged within the real.' No poet is more modest and absolute about such a commitment than Mahon. Maybe *The Winter's Tale* with its images of wreckage/loss and recovery/resurrection, its deeply textured, casual music of a world restored against the odds, is his best emblem. Or maybe he's saving that for his next volume.

    He is (God love him – as my mother would say), a national treasure. Read and see.

Richard Hayes

VARIETIES OF UNEASE

Siobhán Campbell, *Cross-Talk* (Seren Books, 2009), £7.99.
Moyra Donaldson, *Miracle Fruit* (Lagan Press, 2010), £9.99.
Shirley McClure, *Who's Counting?* (Bradshaw Books, 2010), €12.
Kevin Higgins, *Frightening New Furniture* (Salmon Poetry, 2010), €12.
Iggy McGovern, *Safe House* (Dedalus Press, 2010), €11.50.
Damian Smyth, *Lamentations* (Lagan Press, 2010), £8.95.
Damian Smyth, *Market Street* (Lagan Press, 2010), £8.99.

Siobhán Campbell's *Cross-Talk* is a powerful piece of work. Sometimes the poems are angry and defiant, but always there is control, poise, measure: there is real authority through the writing. The book's epigraphs are from Hewitt and MacNeice, Northerners like Campbell, and she shares with them a concern with identity. 'Our genes are thick with doubt', she writes in 'North'; there is a real unease with the place throughout the collection. 'Almost in Sight' brilliantly evokes the strangeness of a summer visit: 'Even the bread is different, comes in rounds, / farls quartered with a steady hand.' The poem considers whether there is 'a line that lets you know your place', that is, a line between the countries, such a line (as the poem tells us) that might tempt a border-guard to slip across and back some night to be able to say: '*I was in Ireland once.*' Repeatedly Campbell seeks to define that line, at least psychologically: her 'cross-talk' is talk about crossing as well as talk that is cross. Her discomfort is a linguistic problem as much as anything; an ancestor advises her in 'Campbell':

> "Though you are from the south, you need to find the will
> to hold a vowel too long. Tell people by their heed
> and know who must be paid. Keep always your own name.
> It takes a softened tongue to fill a twisted mouth."

Campbell avoids the obvious in her treatment of the matter of the North. In 'Troubled', for instance, we read of her 'father's foil. / A cousin once removed' who joined the Irish Guards,

> Played rugby and deck quoits
> On board a ship he built for
> Workman Clark,
> Drank gin with a twist
> Voted for the Communists

> Asked who carried on when Cain finished Abel,
> Had it all to lose
> Never wrote a word.

Then, doubting herself, she asks: 'Or was he that other?' Was he the man, she asks, who brought bad luck on his family by breaking off 'a piece of causeway to keep',

> Smuggled petrol over the border
> Cut growth hormone with talcum powder
> Had three bulls in different fields
> Developed a rare mini-marrow.

One often feels this lightness of touch. In 'The Surprise', for instance, we meet 'A landlady as mean as Ireland in the fifties', who serves one boiled egg ('it's a cooked breakfast, isn't it') under the gaze of 'the red bloom of the Sacred Heart' and 'an airbrushed JFK'. Then this B&B owner delivers the surprise:

> "I must take them down," she says,
> "put Paisley there, Bigfoot though he is, he led,
> and that other fellah, came back to the people in the end
> and handsome enough I suppose, in his own way."

The wry humour does not disguise serious work by a serious poet. This is a fine collection that confidently takes on the tradition of Hewitt, MacNiece and others and makes an original contribution to it.

Unease also dominates Moyra Donaldson's *Miracle Fruit*. In 'Unquiet', she writes of 'the whole chaotic caboodle of my life'. The poem in some ways sets the theme of the book, her second collection; the 'unquiet life', the various disturbances that create life's chaos, are the source of the poetry here. The strong lyric poems that make up the book's central section reverberate most of all with 'unquietness'. 'Barr Hall', one of the more successful poems, could be – is, in some ways – a simple reflection on the meaning of home. But while there is a homeliness established – 'This is my home, this small acreage / and for the first time, I feel at home' – so also we are told that 'I want less and I want more' and 'A colder madness holds me in the stillness / of Cuan my lough of safe haven.' The epigraph, by W H Mearns, to the central section of the book (also called *Unquiet*), sets the tone: 'As I was going up the stair, / I met a man who wasn't there.' These kind of 'present absences' – the home that leaves one wanting less and more, the dead that are evoked in many of the poems, what's missing amidst the daily clutter (in 'Clutter') – haunt the collection's central section.

The first and third sections of the book, respectively *Hunter* and *Circus*, take more formal risks than the poems in *Unquiet*. *Hunter* gathers poems that make reference to John Hunter, an eighteenth-century surgeon, from a range of points of view. So, in 'The Skeleton of the Great Irish Giant', for instance, a giant Irishman dies, is purchased by Hunter, boiled down to bones and displayed in Hunter's museum. Then we hear the skeleton's voice:

> Expendable, all of us, voiceless in death
> as in life, we serve to illustrate. What?

Later on we hear the voice of John Abernethy giving the oration opening the museum in which these skeletons reside. This section of the book is most successful when it stays anchored to Hunter; one suspects more sustained attention to this man, his life and times, the people surrounding him, would have paid greater dividends. *Circus* is more ambitious again and is loosely gathered around pen-portraits of people identified as circus freaks. The first poem – 'Sins of the Fathers' – has a Doctor Munro announce a wonder child, an illegitimate son of a Ms Galloway, 'an astonishing / dispensation of Providence pointing out the truth' – 'the alleged father's name in legible letters in his infant son's right eye.' We meet a Man-Bear ('like a man in shape, / but furred like a bear'), conjoined twins Daisy and Violet ('*Us* is I are Kate Skinner's / unwanted bastard horror'), and a sword swallower. The book ends with 'Dissolution of the Circus' – the big cats have died, the elephant impounded, the clown 'enrolled with the Open University / – English Literature and Philosophy', and now the only two left are the ring-master and the speaker, the acrobat, who – 'though the spangles / have mostly fallen off my costume'— 'can still balance up there on the wire.'

Miracle Fruit is a strong collection, though the quality of the work is inconsistent. The poems drawing on the eighteenth century sometimes flatter to deceive; though the voices evoked are convincing, that 'The Skeleton of the Great Irish Giant', for instance, ends with the skeleton speculating on his illustrative purpose is not a surprise. Stronger are the lyrics at the centre of the book, though these too sometimes become clichéd – railing against Death 'poking his long nose / into my life again' in 'Slievemoyle Love Poem' creates little excitement, for instance. But the poems overall are an unsettling read – expressions of the 'unquietness' informing them, perhaps—and this means, overall, the collection is greater than its parts and a book worth returning to. The fine presentation by Lagan Press is worth noting.

Of all the books reviewed here, Shirley McClure's *Who's Counting?* is the least convincing. Certainly it is an enjoyable collection and, though much in the volume is expected, the handling of various themes and life experiences is witty and at times quite distinctive. The book is in three sections, all the poems personal lyrics. The first section contains largely love poems, of a sort; the second, darker poems, including poems about the experience of cancer; and the third is made up of miscellaneous outward-looking poems about, for instance, working in a London hostel, travel, coffee, cinnamon. While some of the poems verge on the prosaic, there are compensations: there is humour here, and some fine imagery. For instance, 'Before Cancer' begins in a rather pedestrian manner: 'I don't want to think of you / hopeless on a metal bed'; it ends better, however, with the speaker 'bringing you a cupful of snow / from the hospital car park'. 'Ambivalence' just about comes off, its throw-together feel echoing the sentiments of the poem:

> Your nearly-No
> is so, so far
> from my almost-Yes
>
> that if I didn't
> sort of
> know you
>
> I'd practically throw
> my hat
> at happiness.

However, the desperation is not endearing, neither here nor in many of the poems ('Who's Counting?' records that you 'said you loved me / on the sixty-second date'). When that desperation is purely desire, though, the poems work, as in 'Yoga Class' that opens the book where the workman:

> ...inserted the rawl plug,
> then with slightly quicker breath
> he drove it deep
> into my freshly-painted, trembling
> Orchid White walls.

This is a first collection; there is promise here of greater things to come.

Kevin Higgins is prolific: *Frightening New Furniture* is his third collection in five years, after *The Boy with No Face* (2005) and *Time Gentlemen, Please* (2008), both – as here – published by Salmon. And there are over sixty poems in this book. There is a nod to Larkin's 'Dockery and Son' in 'Untidiness' ('life is untidiness / and then only the end / of untidiness'), and Larkin is perhaps a model. Certainly there is something of Larkin in the grouchy pose repeatedly adopted. 'That Was My Country' is somewhat typical: this was a country where, 'Wherever we wanted to go / *Ryanair* would get us almost / there and the world was / not our problem.' Now, he muses,

> We still have butter
> on our *Rich Tea* biscuits
> for now, but no more
> *Coconut Creams*;
> and everywhere statues
> of virgins and freedom fighters
> think about stretching their legs.

'Midnight Mass' is more savage again: 'For one night only, everyone who's anyone / joins everyone who's not' at mass, and when the priest asks the congregation to think about people who have died in the past year, while all other eyes close, the speaker's remain open, examining people who have 'gone nowhere', people he has imagined dying, 'worms having, for starters, / their right eyeballs before moving on to the main course / of brain.'

Higgins has an interest in formal challenges – there are several villanelles in the collection, for instance – and, though lacking Larkin's masterful touch, Higgins generally remains in control. 'Unmade' is an interesting experiment in this regard and is worth quoting in full:

> Paradise has taken a beating.
> Dawn raids on houses I used to live in.
> The ghosts of my unmade friends gather.
> Out for the evening, I end up in a taxi
> the man with curry on his jacket.
> Or, alone with my armchair hatreds,
> I sit here hoping Dick Cheney will phone.
> Dick Cheney will phone I sit here hoping.
> Or, alone with my armchair hatreds,
> the man with curry on his jacket
> I end up in a taxi. The ghosts
> of my unmade friends gather.
> Dawn raids on houses I used to live in.
> Paradise has taken a beating.

The disappointed note is sounded throughout the collection, frequently in the poems that recall various romances that take place against a grim backdrop of 1980s London, or elsewhere. 'Our End of Summer Holiday,

1989' has him 'open the filofax and scribble *cancelled* / across the months I'd
planned / to spend in your pants'. 'This / is where,' he says, 'I slip through /
the non-existent ice.'

The collection's greatest weakness is for editorial control: too many of
the poems seem alike in their complaints, and the tired, sometimes bitter
disappointment becomes wearing. The strengths of some of the better
poems are therefore hidden; a slimmer volume would have brought them
out more. This is unfortunate because Higgins's is a distinctive voice
with a hard edge and plenty of interest to say.

Somewhat in contrast, Iggy McGovern shows himself a poet very much
in control. *Safe House*, his second collection, is a formally adept and well-
rounded book and a pleasure to read. 'The Women in the Moon' is a fine
poem, in its achievement typical of the collection, charting a life through
the women that, at various times, form its centre – the first 'must put /
the food on plates, the clothes on backs'; the second 'is ahead of you /
in everything ... But she minds you in the backlane'; the third 'redeems you
from the thrum / of city-bars and one-night stands'; the fourth,

> is merely waiting to
> complete the quartet that the heavens
> fling into your orbit: she
> will always be your little girl,
> red apple cheeks and bluebell eyes,
> and when she grows you'll be the one
> to sit up till the cows come home,
> complaining, watching for the goose-
> drawn chariots that ferry her
> hither, thither.

The first section of the book, loosely autobiographical, offers many
strong lyric performances such as this one, including a number of very
fine sonnets. 'Sacraments' is a sequence (mostly) of sonnets informed by
the experience of growing up Catholic in the North. Some of these poems
are charming and memorable, like 'Melchizedek', where the photograph
of a priest in the family disappears, with the young speaker later finding
the picture face down in a drawer:

> He came to visit, brought photographs:
> a wife and family, somewhere foreign.
> Marking orders old and new,
> we name him Father Pat-That-Was.

The book's second, short section develops the autobiographical theme
and is again formally ambitious. In the sonnet sequence, 'Letters from

the Captain', the poems take as their basis correspondence between McGovern's grandfather, who was the gardener of a Big House in Tyrone in the 1930s, and his employer, a Captain Joynson-Wreford. The Captain, dying from TB, wrote to Andy McHugh from Davos, advising on and seeking help with the affairs of his estate and, as McGovern writes in a brief note, 'providing a moving remembrance of his abandoned home'. The sequence is marvellous, a wonderful imagining of the Captain's loneliness (in 'The Umbrella' he asks, 'Be with me now, in all that lies ahead – / my boon companion, when all hope is fled'), and his sense of loss (in 'War' he speculates that 'some things will not remain: / small courtesies of life, my lost demesne'). The sequence ends with two brilliant poems that bring McGovern himself into the story. In the first, 'Two Cars', his childhood self finds the Captain's daughter's pedal car in a turf shed and steers it down the road, an echo of the Captain's own (last) departure from the estate in his 'SS', 'the touring vehicle consummate'. And in 'The Pheasants', McGovern considers the stuffed birds 'bought for ten shillings at the closing sale', all that remains of the house.

The third section of *Safe House* is made up of more occasional verse. It retains McGovern's wit and style, though some of the poems ('Proverbs for the Computer Age', for instance) are rather throwaway. Alone these poems would be of passing interest; here, they pale beside the greater achievements of the earlier sections in the book. The centre of gravity in *Safe House* is in 'Letters from the Captain', worth the cover price alone. But there are many very strong poems in this excellent collection.

Of all the books reviewed here, *Lamentations* and *Market Street* by Damian Smyth are the most ambitious, the most interesting. Both display a poet responding remarkably to difficult formal challenges. *Lamentations* is a collection of seventy short poems, rhymed (broadly) *aba bab*; *Market Street* collects longer poems, each of twenty lines, each reflecting on some aspect of life in Downpatrick. There is a wonderful variety of effects achieved by Smyth despite – indeed because of – these formal constraints.

Lamentations seems really a long poem masquerading as a book, though its existence in book form gives the individual sections the breathing space they would not have in long-poem form. The poems – composed, we are told in a note, over several months in the early summer of 2009 – powerfully inter-weave elegies for road-crash victims, people lost in a fishing tragedy, killed in a plane crash, and a number of others (notes at the back offer brief newspaper excerpts giving the background). Poem 50 (there are no titles) recalls the aftermath of a car crash:

It was a task to go back to the site
those few hours later, the warm tarmac rent,
the wound of it bathed in the noon sunlight,

and everything important absent
but his belongings. Bits and bobs, makeweight
the impact forced from the glove compartment.

The poems are directed inwards too, however: 'It's as if every word I
have written / was not already about this, and this / alone', he writes in
34. And in 36 he opens: 'Tonight I am ashamed to be alive.' His feeling are
summed up in 43:

I have a poetry of absences
violently felt. Nothing pastoral
about this landscape of harsh sentences,

nothing sweet or eloquent or floral,
just the zeros of wreaths, the silences
of tongues like small animals gone feral.

There is no relief at the end of the collection. While 'There comes that
point where you begin to reek / of it ... grief, the simple fuel of heartbreak'
('66'), the grief cannot be cast off. 'That event on the road to Emmaus /
promises much', he writes in '67', 'But three deaths later, it's a strange
sojourn / now on the road between the villages.' The book ends with
the seventieth poem:

For these things I weep, my eyes fail with tears.
The badger and the hare, our gentle friends,
shuffling their way on the tarmac frontiers,

not making it before the journey ends;
the peacock struck in the street unawares;
three coffins for a while in these two hands.

This profound and moving collection charts the journey towards the
realisation that in the end there is perhaps only surrender to the inevitability
of loss.

Market Street is as formally constrained as Lamentations. It is a less
unified collection, thematically at least, though it does draw a different
kind of unity from geography. The book's table of contents is effectively
a list of shops and people in Downpatrick, and so we have poems like 'A
Fruit Bowl from Down Jewellers' next to 'A Scythe from Hugh Kelly' and,
further along, 'A Haircut from Tommy Miley' side-by-side with 'A Lotion
from Superdrug', or 'A Down Recorder from Charlie Rourke' with 'A
Round at the Golf Course'. The effort here is familiar enough: 'It's the

mundane conclusion: the fantastic is everywhere', we read in 'A Telescope from Kerr & Belshaw'. Certainly the book makes strange the mundane – a shopping trip down a provincial street becomes a fantastic, celebratory set of meditations on history and identity. But the collection has greater ambition than this kind of defamiliarisation. Several times in the book a sunken ship appears, the wreckage shifting with the tide. *Market Square* takes its energy from this image, it seems: time passes in the town, people come and go, are glimpsed then hidden like the wreck: 'Whole histories set aside as if they never were' ('A Schooner from the East Downshire Steamship Co'). Personalities, past and present, appear and re-appear. 'A Rector in Killyleagh', for instance, draws a lovely portrait of Edward Hincks, the rector of the title and also a consultant for the British Museum, who is pictured here, 'hoop-backed over his desk like a gryphon', deciphering drawings from an archeological find in nineteenth-century Iraq and finding there 'something like footprints in the sand and he is afraid they are his own.' He reappears later, 'tired of the Age' ('A Visit from Reverend Hincks') and inevitably too the Rector passes into oblivion; Smyth's note on 'A Rector in Killyleagh' reproduces his own letter to the *London Review of Books* (January 2009) that remembers Hincks's largely-forgotten contribution to the study of ancient civilisation and seeks to find a place for him again. In these circumstances, a wrench ('A Wrench from McMaster's'), a newspaper ('A *Belfast Telegraph* from Malachi O'Doherty'), boots ('A Pair of Boots from McCartan's') survive and come to form evidence of human existence. The book does not simply then seek to reveal the marvellous in the local but also to denote the town's inevitable passing. There are contemporaries also evoked here, such as in 'A Cortège for Jean McConville', a desperately sad lament for the woman from whom the earth took everything 'without unbuttoning a blouse or slipping a single hook from an eye.' The abiding sense is of humans passing through history and leaving little enough behind to recall that passing. The poems in *Market Square* are glossed by a set of notes from Smyth as intriguing and interesting as the poems themselves – they make up almost a third of the book. The book also contains an eccentric index that, in a sense, is the book in summary (and is arguably a poem in its own right): *Market Square* aims to chart a multi-dimensional geography for not just the town but for life itself. So we have multiple entries for 'light', 'place', 'earth'; entries for 'St Dillon's Well', 'Vietnam', 'Tommy Miley', 'Skeffington's''; and entries for 'cordite', 'brucellosis', 'porphyry', 'monsters (of a kind)', 'using the skull as a cast', 'Ireland' and 'your whole self'.

Market Square is unlike anything else in recent Irish poetry. Together with *Lamentations*, it shows Damian Smyth as an ambitious poet with formidable gifts. This is work to be treasured.

Catherine Toal

TRANSITIONAL STYX

Sara Berkeley, *The View from Here* (Gallery Press, 2010), €11.95.
Peter Sirr, *The Thing Is* (Gallery Press, 2009), €11.95.
Fiona Sampson, *Rough Music* (Carcanet, 2010), £9.95.

From her début *Penn* in 1986, Sara Berkeley's poems have always drawn
the reader in through the enunciation or the implied presence of a
biographical 'I' which undergoes dramatic metamorphoses, even managing
to dissolve imperceptibly into abstraction. This feature takes on a particular
power in her latest collection, which is preoccupied with retrospective
reflection on the phases of life, and with death, mourning and memory.
A number of the poems become variations on the positions from which
death can be imagined. Paradigmatically, 'Warm Bodies, Cold Bodies'
portrays the death by drowning of the son of a neighbouring couple (his
mother's perspective becomes the first-person of the subsequent 'Aquifer'),
by fusing their daily recollection of it with a description of the event
itself. The last lines, tracing his impulse to go into the sea, the idea of the
departure as an inevitable rebellion and dispossession, as well as an
image the parents have of him as a child, show Berkeley's compaction of
competing emotional and temporal perspectives within a single sequence:

> In his kick-down deckchair
> he feels the tidal pull, and it makes sense
> to let his moorings loose,
> he who used to have prayers,
> someone to say them to,
> a way of kneeling before the bed.

As if inhabiting the subjectivity of the lost son, 'Where He Is Now' paints
a disabused experience of the process itself ('He thought death would be
all altitude. / Instead, this languorous drown'). With a generalised
allegorical device familiar from several of the lyrics, one that destroys
atomised individual point of view, an exhortatory speech from the figure
'Life' asks the dying man to think of himself as other people he has
encountered, rather than as the sum of his own recollections. 'All Souls
Passing Over' presents a vision of the allegorical through the everyday,
Berkeley's unpretentiousness creating a sense of the ominous, the
unavoidable and the absurd in this encounter with an unidentified Charon:
'you also know // that faint splashing to be the oars of some / ferryman

who rises out of the mist [...] / / and takes from his pocket something meaningful, / like a key that unlocks the gate you have been / gazing at the garden through since you were little.'

'Shelter', 'Meals for Friends', 'Park Bench, Queens', and 'Ghost, Soho' all play with the juxtaposition between living and being actually or effectively dead, nullifying the difference between them to generate an ambiguous reassertion of life, as in the most beautiful and devastating lyric of the book, 'The Angel of Poetry'. 'Untwinned' provides an unusual, grisly instance of this juxtaposition, with a burlesque childhood murder, a vision of willed spiritual extinction, and a final scene of grief, whose factual, abbreviated terms are a poignant slang for the hard-headedness of the collection's confrontation with loss and suffering: 'some loads / are too much / for the strongest ventricles; / / some packs too heavy / for even the bravest girls.' In 'The Influence of Ghosts', where youth, continuing the series of fundamental, reversible oppositions that orders the collection, has 'altitude', the temptation to suicide is likewise given both its painfulness and its typical melodrama through a biological reference: 'My cells / cried out in unison, *abandon us! abandon us!*' The poem, again through the introduction of another voice, like that of the authoritative supernal figures ('Life', 'Poetry') elsewhere manifested, subtly inculcates an acceptance of loss: 'The secret is, / at last, that losing every-thing / / makes perfect sense. It cannot be / another way.' 'It' as opposed to 'There' in this last line, apparently indefinite (like the 'something meaningful' of the 'All Souls Passing Over' poem), refers to 'way' rather than to an abstract idea, and in its consequent effect of imbecility articulates a child-like rather than a doomed sense of limitation. In '59th Street Bridge' the narrator, contemplating suicide in defiance of a pursuer, again deploys the poignant (and perverse) power of this infantine element (invoking as well the earlier scenario of a child's death by drowning): 'I will do as all children of the sea are born to do: / stay out there until dinner is no longer being served'. The final poems of the collection transform this simplicity into a hymnal and ritual quality, 'Absolution', 'Rain at Easter' and 'This I Take With Me'. Their colloquial frankness and sporadic rhymes produce a quality of reassurance but also a deliberately jarring, unreliable element, as in the last poem, 'Boathouse', where the Styx is never far away, despite the final affirmation of 'This. Here. Now.'

Perhaps it's the sense of a current national need for defiant vitriol, but it's difficult not to be particularly struck by the references in Peter Sirr's *The Thing Is* to the present situation in Ireland. In this collection full of lists, we find a catalogue of unhappy citizens in 'Shhh': 'and no one much is smiling now, not the firemen / / nor the baggage handlers, nurses, first time buyers / and since they changed the city boundaries and lowered the fares / / my taxi driver's blue with rage, who never asked anyone to live in Celbridge / or fucking Maynooth'. Imitations of the invective of Catullus produce the fragment: 'It's not the winds that blast / your country retreat / but the squalls of an endless mortgage./ How long can it last? / *Myhome.ie*, thousands of houses / decades of unrest' ('Carmina'). In fact, the problems of predictability and historical dead-ends are central to the formal concern of the collection: the impossibility of truly generating and experiencing poetic originality. This is already clear in the obstinate directness of the dedicatory poem (called simply 'An Opening') which offers itself 'For everything, for nothing', delineating a supplementary list – 'for the thinning trees / for ditches / for watery fields' – whose significance seems to be that of exhausting all possibilities in order to start completely anew. It is also suggested by the treatment of the forebears Sirr chooses to name: 'Music for Viols' cites listening to Jordi Savall's playing of Tobias Hume's 'Good Againe', as if the seventeenth-century composer is not fully accessible through his twentieth-century rendering: 'and walk in / as far as the tune will go.' Brecht's 'O Lust des Beginnens!', a perhaps parodic apostrophe to the as-yet unformed lyric idea, becomes in Sirr's rewriting ('Ode to Beginning') a sober litany and careful set of reminders. Similarly, the poem for Jules Supervielle ('Le Regret De La Terre') mourns a lost capacity for poetic concreteness, either represented or itself once yearned for by the deceased renegade surrealist.

In their own innovations, the poems explore a variety of methods for defeating the deadness of formula – often by actively exploiting it. For instance, the longer poem sequences 'Shhh' and 'The Overgrown Path' juxtapose pseudo-scientific sloganising ('tunable munitions, psychotronics, voice to skull technologies') with sparser elegiac lyric modes. In a second prominent motif, the language of children appears both as purely imitative and a as a source of freshness. 'Concert Going' (part of 'The Overgrown Path') links the teaching of speech to the familiar milestones of literary history, and to the known tricks of the poem itself: 'hello black cat dark yard sudden / semantic flurry [...] / this is your mouth / where the food goes / like Shakespeare to his theatre'. 'Poem', from the same series, forms itself out of the real time of its making, 'wanting' at its end to become one with the child's voice 'to sing / the bright music of our daughter', which it can only do by orthographic addendum '(this line is written in her laughter)'. The brilliant poem of the collection's title captures the jubilance of that unoriginal moment of a child showing those typical drawings to her father: 'miraculous: you're pure crayon, nothing but crayon now.'

The effects are most fascinating when Sirr considers the problem of original rendering in relation to the slow assembling of a landscape or an image, as in 'The Different Rains Come Down'. The gathering complexity of its final stanzas figures a wren at the edge of grassland in a way that recalls the ludic identification of states of consciousness and a hypothetical scene in Wallace Stevens's 'Thirteen Ways of Looking at A Blackbird'. Rather than making the condition of thinking equivalent to the arrangement of a picture, Sirr's last two lines evoke the experience of the mind's fixation on an image, the mind-body split itself, and the possibility that the mind overwhelms the image with thought: 'but standing there like nothing at all, / a post brushed by moth-wings, / a stillness rent with little cries, / a body thinned to bone like a hook / the mind might throw its hat on and forget.' 'Here You Are' operates like a telescope or camera trying to find its view, capturing the surprise of what it sees by losing and regaining sight of its elements, in a manner that both pays tribute to the typicality of the joy it celebrates, and acknowledges the impossibility of representing it for the first time: 'the dog on his extendable lead / extending himself out of view / here are // your badly recorded voices singing / [...] /here you are // disposed in light / and the company of trees / and here am I, applauding.'

Fiona Sampson's *Rough Music* seems in form at least not to live up to its title; the poems are flawlessly smooth syncopations of sound as well as arabesque configurations of fluid movement. For example, the first line of the commentary provided by 'The Code', *We have discovered the secret of life* (the famous quotation from Francis Crick, identifying this as the code patterning all life), rounds itself by running the gamut of vowel sounds between a beginning and an end 'o', thereby linking the scientific explanation ('how') to the microcosmic totality it discovers ('whole'). In its middle the line gives substantiality to the objects examined and illuminated, in the sounds 'ch', 'th', 'th.' The stanzas that follow use a variety of devices to parallel the concept of a latent completeness in living forms, and the paradox of a knowledge that is both hidden and now generalised.

It is in its thematic allusions to violence, isolation and suffering that the collection earns its reference to the practice of popular ritual mockery that involved musical or other entertainment. The Classical dialogues it includes suggest contemporary scenarios of rape, murder, abandonment. Two of its sparsest poems, 'Crow Voodoo' and 'Blade' perform their lyric and stanzaic manoeuvres around the idea of mutilation by a knife. 'Crow Voodoo' gestures towards the aftermath of violation in its final image, 'light scars / the retina', of the body awakening to its wounds. In 'Blade' the exclusion of the actual moment of attack from representation is given a more titillating, delectable quality: 'A whisper / of tongue', the last phrase, signals the first signs of disturbance in the female body under assault.

What mars the effectiveness of Sampson's combination of lyric elegance with wrenching subject-matter is not the incongruity between the two, but other instances of allusion that disrupt onomatopoeic pattern and the ingenious unfurling of motion. In 'Zeus to Juno' (a strange Greek-Roman coupling in any case), the 'She' voice begins 'You were taboo / not totem'; the evocation of a Freud book title makes the distinction sound ludicrous, even if the terminological opposition makes sense as one between prohibited, sublime power and worshipped idol or fetish. 'At Käsmu' seems the most difficult to assimilate of the poems, not because of the complexity of its references; Sampson tends to translate poetic philosophical theories into prose: 'what's in question is how to inhabit / (an identity, a place) fully, /which for Heidegger meant without reflection.' The obstacle lies rather in the apparent lack of urgency of the issues it raises, and the banality with which they are surveyed: 'Or (to try it another way, / as evening cools outside the open window) / why should I finally face / the problem of identity / on this Baltic peninsula, / surrounded by an unknown language/sweet as birdcall?' The appearance of a group of swans towards the end of the poem seems to offer an opportunity to return to seamless combinations of physical image, lyric suppleness and implicit idea, but Sampson relapses into direct, trite state-ment: 'though I dream of something fixed, / history completes me too'. Yet more unremarkable is the casual liberality of the parting assertion: 'I love whatever changes.'

Where Sampson's poetry achieves greatest memorability is in an ironic combination of the theme of suffering and a parodic use of perfect poetic shape. 'From the Adulteress's Songbook', a ditty that gives the impression of coming from a medieval chapbook or Chaucerian character-portrait, is itself a commentary on the voiding of meaning from form, where marriage is dissolved of its substance because of a mismatch between the object of feeling and the duties imposed by the institution. Similarly, 'Vigil', a reverse-prayer or curse upon the self, achieves its impact through an incantatory rhyme whose formulaic quality has an anomalous relationship to the power of its own content. In 'From the Adulteress's Songbook', this feature emerges in the painful stumble the rhyme takes towards and away from the 'warmth' vanished from the speaker's experi-ence: 'and wandered out among the forms / that might inform a life, / finding cold comfort in each warmth / because I was a wife.' In 'Vigil', the impetus to purge and punish anger offers a harsh syllable's candidacy for hackneyed repetition:

> You whose daylight
> thrills the nerves –
> burn me now
> as I deserve.

Michael O'Loughlin

THUNDERBIRDS ARE GO!

Alan Moore, *How Now!* (Anvil Press, 2010), £8.95.
Mark Granier, *Fade Street* (Salt Publishing, 2010), hb £12.99.

How Now? Good question. One often asked by the middle-aged poet
who finds himself in the middle of the dark wood, beset by drink,
divorce, depression, and the usual plethora of ills. From Dante to Lowell
to Durcan, it has been a fine spur to inspiration, and it is this tradition
that Alan Moore looks to. The answer, of course, to how we have become
what we are now, lies in our childhoods, and like *Life Studies* and *Daddy,
Daddy, How Now!* is haunted by spectres of flawed male role models. Mad
Ireland hurt those men, and they, in their turn, hurt us. Enough
psychoanalysis, what about the poetry?

   Alan Moore burst onto the poetry scene in 1986 with his first book
Opia, a prizewinning virtuoso display that seemed to have little connection
to other Irish poetry at the time. Superficially, its extreme metaphors and
polished surfaces, its vacuum-packed emotions, seemed to place it in the
orbit of the so-called 'Martian poets'. (Does anyone remember them?).
His taste for the Martian metaphor has not faded, as in 'Now':

> Like Hueys over Vietnam,
> My toothbrush wages war on plaque and cavities.

In *How Now!* this technique is in the service of serious emotional issues,
and not just an aesthetic effect. The problem raised by *Opia* was, where
was there left for the poet to go after such a perfect performance? This, his
second book, provides the answer. To begin with, nowhere: the strange
wasteland that was Ireland in the 1980s and 1990s, a country which was
ceasing to be one thing, without knowing what it would become.

   Another aspect of *Opia* which survives is the poet's novelist-style
appetite for the surface of things, the details, the cultural minutiae of a
1960s Irish suburban childhood. The USA biscuit tin, Pan's People, Austin
Cambridges and Anglias, Thunderbirds wallpaper, will evoke emotions in
everyone of a certain age.

   But these Anglo-American cultural signifiers float on the dark, stagnant
pond of Irish family life:

> Daddy sits on the bed, surrounded by his bills.
> "What the fuck do *you* want?" he says.
> I see fear in his bloodshot eyes.
>   – 'FAMILY TIME'

And, from 'Chorley':

> Daddy gives Mammy her present.
> A leather bag. Her eyes are like the Hood.
> She beats him on the head with it.

The deadpan, affectless tone of these childhood poems makes them all the more disturbing. Moore has no designs on the reader. The vignettes are presented in an almost forensic fashion, it is up to us to fill in the missing emotions, which have been blanked by alcohol, repression, conformity. Sex rears its beautiful head in slightly unusual forms:

> "Undress," the Gestapo officer tells Nina.
> She strips and stands in silence with
> Her back to us. He examines her clothes.
> "What is he looking for?" I ask.
> Both my parents have suddenly gone deaf.
> — 'GLENDOHER'

Truly, there was no sex in Ireland before television. But outside the home too, more fear and brutality await:

> "Put out your hand," he says. *Swoop. Swoop.*
> "The other one,' he says. *Swoop. Swoop.*
> James Connolly seems satisfied.
> Patrick Pearse looks away.
> — 'TEACHERS'

As Moore escapes from the grasp of the Christian Brothers and out into the workaday world of the civil service, things are not much better. Moore sardonically evokes the everyday horror and hatred of the office:

> My boss shows me to the Sorting Office.
> His breath reeks of whiskey.
> A postman deals letters to open-mouthed sacks.
> 'You're only a bollix, Murphy," he says.
> "Who is he talking to?" I ask.
> "Never mind," my boss says.
> — 'CIVIL SERVICE'

How to counter this emotional emptiness? The poet turns to culture. He memorises King Lear, listens to Mozart and Pink Floyd, and the handy anaesthetic of alcohol is always within reach ('Alcohol and Me'):

> Guinness like oil in the spill trays.
> Behind, a row of teats:
> Paddy, Huzzar, Teachers.

But that old sow proves as treacherous as the Joycean one. However, by the end of the book, the tone of the poems is accepting and almost joyful. The final poem, 'Oblivion', a fine valedictory to the body which sustains us, ends:

> Hard to believe the world is about to
> Have its first day in my absence.

Having come through, having exorcised his demons to some extent, it will be fascinating to see where Moore goes from here.

When reviewing books together it is always tempting to look for points of comparison. And though Mark Granier is very different, he is of an age with Alan Moore and shares, as is inevitable, some of the same cultural baggage. He too revisits the casual brutality of the Irish suburban childhood in decades gone by:

> It flashes back like an outtake: my nine-year-old flight
> down a lengthening dim corridor,
> those quiet words spoken by the doctor
>
> snapping at my feet: 'I can circumcise you now, if you like.'
> – 'FALSE MEMORY'

Childhood is not a major theme in the book, even though the book is permeated with a subdued sadness, an awareness of the transience of things, a constant underlying expectation of imminent disaster, like a distant hum, which may have its roots in childhood experience. Granier's poetic objectives are different. He is very much a poet of individual poems, whereas Moore's book functions more as a whole, and this is both the strength and possible weakness of *Fade Street*. His poems are often perfectly operating verbal machines, which are their own fulfilment, with everything concentrated on the final, sealing line. Often this is extremely effective, as in 'Naylor's Cove', an intimation of mortality:

>   ...Atomised eyes
> level and look straight through
>
> your own, unfocusing, till you know nothing but the air
> that stares you so thoroughly out.

Granier is nothing if not self-aware of his own practice, and even handles it in a joking fashion in a poem like 'Don't End with History Or The Sea' (famous advice from Kenneth Koch). However, it can also have a slightly suffocating effect, which can exclude the reader. Granier is well-known for his visual sense, and the poems often have the effect of a fixed image.

> A framed, blown-up photograph hangs on the wall:
> the t-shirted butcher's son and his wife, on their honeymoon
> in Manhattan, the towers in the background, the date:
> September 10, 2001.'
>
> – 'AT THE BUTCHER'S IN COLMENAR'

Suggestive as this is, there is a danger here. *Ut Pictura Poesis*: poems are made of pictures, we know, but they are also made of language, which is ultimately more ambiguous and open to different interpretations than the visual. I would warm to some of these poems more if they were a little rougher around the edges. However, the visual and verbal precision of a poem such as 'A Photograph of Fade Street, Dublin, 1878' is impressive, bearing witness to a rigorous, dogged, attention to the real which is rare enough in poetry: 'dark fanlights / / above dark doors, sash windows raised / while the far end assumes its name, greys / to a smoky membrane.'

There are other sides to Granier too. Some of the poems I found most enjoyable in the book indulged a kind of zany surrealism, like 'A Chest Of Drawers', or the more straightforward humour of 'One of the Houses James Joyce Lived In, Once':

> James Joyce ivy
> on James Joyce plaque,
> James Joyce pebbles
> on James Joyce dash.

This strain is also continued in the effective 'Three Riddles And a Limerick', and I hope he continues to develop it.

These two books can easily claim to be two of the more accomplished, even groundbreaking, books of poetry by Irish poets in the last couple of years. Yet, you will look in vain for these poets in recent anthologies or studies of Irish poetry. Why is this? Is it their lack of interest in the anecdotal, the sense of place, the mythological? Whatever the answer may be, they are evidence of the rude health of Irish poetry beyond what is sometimes seen as the mainstream, and should be read by all interested in contemporary Irish poetry.

Notes on Contributors

Gary Allen's latest collection *Ha, Ha* is forthcoming this year from Lagan Press. His poems are published in *Irish Pages, Edinburgh Review, Poetry Review, Stand, The Yellow Nib*, and elsewhere.

Stuart Barnes lives in Melbourne, Australia. His poetry has been published in a variety of print and online journals, exhibited, and anthologised. He's currently editing his first two chapbooks: *Uprising* (the hazards of psychiatry, the lies of the New World Order); and *Songs from the Edge of the World* (emotional, physical and spiritual responses to HIV and treatment).

Sean Borodale's *Note for an Atlas*, published by Isinglass in 2003, is a book-length topographical poem 'written whilst walking through London'.

Zoë Brigley won an Eric Gregory Award in 2003, and published her début collection of poetry, *The Secret*, with Bloodaxe in 2007. She co-edited *Feminism, Literature and Rape Narratives* for Routledge in 2009.

Liam Carson is Director of the IMRAM Irish Language Literature Festival. His memoir, *Call Mother A Lonely Field*, is published by Hag's Head Press.

Kate Dempsey has published poems in *THE SHOp, Coffeehouse, Orbis, Magma* and in *The Backyards of Heaven: An Anthology of Contemporary Poetry from Ireland and Newfoundland and Labrador*. Her poem 'Amsterdam Otto Recommends', published in this issue, won the short poem category of the online Plough Prize in 2010 (**theploughprize.co.uk**).

Lynley Edmeades has had poems published in her native New Zealand in *JAAM* magazine and in the literary journal *Sport*. She is studying for a M.A. in Creative Writing at Queen's University Belfast.

Andrew Elliott's collection *Lung Soup* was published in 2009 by Blackstaff Press.

Jonathan Ellis is Senior Lecturer in American Literature at the University of Sheffield. He is the author of *Art and Memory in the Work of Elizabeth Bishop* (Ashgate, 2006), as well as articles and essays on Paul Muldoon, Sylvia Plath, and Anne Stevenson. His next book is on twentieth-century letter writing.

Tom French's collections *Touching the Bones* (2001) and *The Fire Step* (2009) are published by Gallery Press. In 2010 he edited *A Meath Anthology* (Meath County Library), and an essay 'The Hummingbird of Athboy' appeared in the 2010 *John McGahern Yearbook*.

Eamon Grennan's latest collections are *Out of Breath* (Gallery Press), and, in the United States, *Out of Sight: New and Selected Poems*. He taught in Vassar college for many years, and currently teaches in the graduate writing programme of Columbia University. He lives in Poughkeepsie, New York, and spends as much time as he can in the West of Ireland.

Kerry Hardie has published two novels with Harper Collins. Her *Selected Poems* was published earlier this year by Gallery Press.

Richard Hayes is Assistant Registrar at Waterford Institute of Technology. He has published a number of articles on contemporary Irish writing and has compiled an index and introduction to *Poetry Ireland Review* (volumes 1-21).

Ron Houchin has recently published poems in *Now & Then*, *New Mexico Poetry Review* and *MOTIF 2: An Anthology of Writings about Chance*. He has published four books – the latest, *Museum Crows*, was published in 2009 by Salmon Poetry.

Benjamin Keatinge is Head of English at the South East European University, Tetovo, Republic of Macedonia. He holds a doctorate on Samuel Beckett from Trinity College Dublin. With co-author Aengus Woods he published a volume of critical essays on poet Brian Coffey, *Other Edens: The Life and Work of Brian Coffey* (Irish Academic Press, 2009).

Nick Laird's poetry collections are *To a Fault* (Faber and Faber, 2005) and *On Purpose* (Faber and Faber, 2007), winner of the Somerset Maugham Award and the Geoffrey Faber Memorial Prize.

Seán Lysaght's collections include *The Clare Island Survey* (1991) and *The Mouth of a River* (2007), both from Gallery Press. His *Robert Lloyd Praeger, the life of a naturalist 1865–1953* was published by Four Courts Press in 1998. His *Selected Poems* is now available from Gallery Press.

Kathy Mac's *Nail Builders Plan for Strength and Growth* (Roseway, 2002) won the Lampert Award for best first book of poems published in Canada. She teaches Creative Writing at Saint Thomas University in Fredericton, New Brunswick, Canada.

John McAuliffe's third book of poetry, *Of All Places*, will be published by Gallery Press in July. He teaches poetry at the Centre for New Writing at the University of Manchester.

Derek Mahon's *New Collected Poems*, an updated version of *Collected Poems* (1999), will be published this year by Gallery Press.

Tom Mathews is a poet, critic and cartoonist who lives and works in Dublin. His first collection, *The Owl and the Pussycat* (Dedalus Press, 2009), was shortlisted for the Rupert and Eithne Strong Award and the Seamus Heaney Prize.

Luke Morgan is a poet based in Co Galway. His poetry has been published in *Crannóg*, in *Writing4all: The Best Of 2009*, and online at *Outburst* (**outburstmagazine.com**) and *The Smoking Poet (*thesmokingpoet.net*)*. He is a senior-cycle student at Coláiste Éinde.

Annemarie Ní Churreáin is a native Irish speaker with a degree in Communication Studies from Dublin City University, and a M. Phil in Creative Writing from the Oscar Wilde Centre, Trinity College Dublin. She is working towards a first collection.

Lauren Norton teaches poetry at the University of California Davis where she is a graduate student in the creative writing program. Her stories and songs are free to download at **thesouterrain.com**.

Jean O'Brien won the 2010 Arvon International Poetry Award. Her most recent collection is *Lovely Legs* (Salmon Poetry, 2009); a new collection, *Love Handles,* is forthcoming this year. She holds a M.Phil in Creative Writing from Trinity College Dublin and tutors in the Irish Writers' Centre.

Killian O'Donnell has published poetry in *New Irish Writing, The Honest Ulsterman, The Dublin Magazine, The Stinging Fly,* and elsewhere.

Mary O'Donnell's sixth poetry collection, *The Ark Builders*, was published by Arc Publications in 2009. She has published three novels and two short story collections and last year edited *To the Winds Our Sails*, an anthology of Galician poetry in translation. She currently teaches poetry at NUI Maynooth. For further information, visit **maryodonnell.com**

Michael O'Loughlin's most recent collection, *In This Life*, is published by New Island.

Paul Perry's most recent books include *The Last Falcon and Small Ordinance* (Dedalus Press, 2010) and *108 Moons: The Selected Poems of Jurga Ivanauskaitė* (The Workshop Press, 2010).

John Redmond is a Senior Lecturer at the University of Liverpool. His latest poetry collection is *MUDe* (Carcanet, 2008) and his study of contemporary poets, *Poetry and Privacy*, is due from Seren in 2012.

Thomas Dillon Redshaw published poems in numerous Irish, British, and American journals in the 1970s. He has one book – *Heimaey* (Dolmen Press, 1974) – and several American chapbooks to his name, as well as numerous scholarly articles on Irish poetry, Irish small presses, and the Dolmen Press. He edited *Well Dreams: Essays on John Montague* (2004).

Edward Reilly has published several poetry chapbooks, a travelogue and critical essays. His M.A. (Deakin University, 1989) was on Thomas Kinsella and Ph.D (Victoria University, 2000) was in Poetics. His poems have appeared in *Nimrod* (Tulsa), *Rio Grande Review* (El Paso), *SideWalk* (Adelaide), *Eureka Street* (Melbourne) and *Literatura ir Menas* (Vilnius).

J S Robinson was educated in biology at Trinity College Dublin and the California Institute of Technology, USA. Her work has been featured in *Poet's Bookshelf*, *The Stinging Fly*, *Census*, *Southword* and the *Sunday Tribune*. Robinson was also a runner up for the Gregory O'Donoghue prize and is preparing her first collection.

Gerard Smyth was born in Dublin where he still lives. His poetry has appeared in publications in Ireland, Britain and America, as well as in translation, since the late 1960s. He is the author of seven collections, the most recent of which is *The Fullness of Time: New and Selected Poems* (Dedalus Press, 2010). He is a member of Aosdána.

Donna Sørensen, originally from the UK, has spent most of the last ten years living in mainland Europe and North America. She currently works for The O'Brien Press in Dublin. Her poems have appeared in *Southword*, *The Stinging Fly* and *Wordlegs*, and she been selected to appear in the Poetry Ireland Introductions Series 2011.

Catherine Toal teaches literature at the European College of Liberal Arts, Berlin.

S D Tucker's first novel, *The Great Pan is Not Dead,* is published by Olympia.